Maria Parloa

First Principles of Household Management and Cookery

A Text Book for Schools and Families

Maria Parloa

First Principles of Household Management and Cookery
A Text Book for Schools and Families

ISBN/EAN: 9783744785921

Printed in Europe, USA, Canada, Australia, Japan

Cover: Foto ©Lupo / pixelio.de

More available books at **www.hansebooks.com**

FIRST PRINCIPLES

OF

HOUSEHOLD MANAGEMENT

AND

COOKERY.

A Text-Book for Schools and Families.

BY

MARIA PARLOA.

NEW AND ENLARGED EDITION.

BOSTON
HOUGHTON, MIFFLIN AND COMPANY
New York: 11 East Seventeenth Street
The Riverside Press, Cambridge
1882

PREFACE.

THE object of this little volume is to spread a knowledge of the common things of every-day life among all the people. Physicians, and others qualified to give an opinion, testify that the foundation for disease, intemperance, and crime is nearly always impure air and water, food improperly cooked, or uncleanly and disorderly homes. The author has long had a desire to help remedy these evils, and while studying the South Kensington, and the Board Schools in London, in 1878, was convinced that the English people had solved the question as to how and where the reform should begin.

In the city of London there are twenty-one practice kitchens, where girls of eleven years of age and upward are sent for practice lessons in the preparation of the plainest dishes. Before these lessons, however, they study a manual of the composition of food, and the principles underlying its preparation. They also learn the simplest rules for the care of the body and dwelling. The schools have been in successful operation for several years, and have done a wonderful amount of good. The same method is followed with marked effect in the manufacturing and mining districts.

After seeing all this, the determination was taken to write a book that could be used in the schools and families of America with like beneficial results. In this work the aim has been to state clearly the causes of disease and the prevention of the same through sanitary laws; the order of household work; the composition and preparation of food, with sick-room cookery; and to give a few hints on the care of the sick. In treating subjects of such importance, it has been difficult to decide what to omit, and yet make the work complete; but the kind reception of the Appledore Cook-Book and the author's New Cook-Book leads to the hope that this volume may, too, find favor with the public.

. . . .

The additional receipts that appear in the last part of the book were chiefly suggested by experience in teaching classes of working women, and are designed especially to benefit those people to whom economy in cooking is a necessity.

NOTE TO THE TEACHER.

Six dishes are all that can be cooked in a lesson. That the pupils might be able to prepare a variety of food in their own homes, more than that number has been given.

The teacher will use her judgment in selecting from each lesson.

CONTENTS.

HOUSEHOLD MANAGEMENT.

CHAPTER I.
THE AIR WE BREATHE 1

CHAPTER II.
THE HOUSE WE LIVE IN 5

CHAPTER III.
THE WATER WE USE 8

CHAPTER IV.
HOUSE WORK 14
General Work. — Washing, Starching, and Ironing. — Fires. — Lamps.

CHAPTER V.
THE HUMAN BODY 26
Analogies of the Steam-Engine and the Living Body. — Composition of the Human Body. — Elements of the Human Body.

CHAPTER VI.

PHYSIOLOGICAL AND CHEMICAL CLASSIFICATION OF
FOOD 31
Albuminous Matters. — Meat. — Milk. — Eggs.

CHAPTER VII.

FISH 38
Boiling, Broiling, Frying. — Baking, Salting. — Lobsters.
— Oysters.

CHAPTER VIII.

VEGETABLES 41
Potatoes. — Turnips. — Squash. — Beets. — Cabbage. — Onions. — Sweet Potatoes. — Tomatoes. — Pease. — Beans. — Carrots. — Parsnips. — Salads.

CHAPTER IX.

FRUITS 45
Apples, Figs, Dates, Bananas.

CHAPTER X.

THE BREAD WE EAT 46
Wheat, New and Old Process. — Graham. — Indian Corn. — Oatmeal. — Rye. — Rice. — Pearled Barley. — Buckwheat. — Bread Making. — How Bread changes in the Baking. — Leaven. — Salt-Rising Bread. — Aerated Bread. — Baking Powders.

CHAPTER XI.

THE CONDIMENTS, SPICES, AND FLAVORS WE USE . 56
Condiments (Salt, Pepper, Mustard). — Spices (Ginger, Nutmeg, Cinnamon, Clove, Mace, Allspice). — Flavors (Lemon, Orange, Vanilla, Bitter Almond).

CHAPTER XII.

TEA, COFFEE, CHOCOLATE, ETC. 61
Tea. — Coffee. — Boiled Coffee. — Filtered Coffee. — Steamed Coffee. — Cocoa. — Chocolate.

COOKERY.

FIRST LESSON.

BREAD AND YEAST 67
Hop Yeast. — Yeast Bread. — Hints on Bread Making. — Graham Bread.

SECOND LESSON.

Beef Stew. — Dumplings. — Roast Meat. — Broiling. — Boiled Potatoes. — Graham Muffins. — Bread Pudding. — Cream Sauce 74

THIRD LESSON.

Pot-au-Feu. — Baked Fish. — Tomato Soup. — Potato Soup. — Baked Indian Pudding 81

FOURTH LESSON.

Meat Hash. — Fish Balls. — Fish Hash. — Oatmeal Mush. — Hominy. — Minute Pudding. — Vinegar Sauce. — Brown Bread 85

FIFTH LESSON.

Fish Chowder. — Beef Olives. — Veal Olives. — Boiled Rice Pudding. — Baked Rice Pudding. — Apple Dowdy. — Lemon Sauce 89

SIXTH LESSON.

Soft Molasses Gingerbread. — Sponge-Cake. — Cream Pies. — Filling for Cream Pies. — Washington Pies. — Whitpot Pudding. — Vegetables. — Time-Table for Cooking Vegetables 94

SEVENTH LESSON.

Salads. — French Salad Dressing. — Boiled Salad Dressing. — Vegetable Salad. — Potato Salad. — Lettuce Salad. — Rich Salad Dressing. — Lobster Salad. — Chicken Salad. — Baked Beans. — Stewed Beans 98

EIGHTH LESSON.

POULTRY 103

To clean Poultry. — Roast Turkey. — Roast Chicken. — Roast Goose. — Roast Duck. — Roast Partridges. — Roast Grouse. — Roast Pigeons. — Small Birds.

NINTH LESSON.

SAUCES 107

Drawn Butter. — Egg Sauce. — Oyster Sauce. — Celery Sauce. — Caper Sauce. — Mint Sauce. — Cream Sauce. — Bread Sauce for Game. — Tomato Sauce. — Hollandaise Sauce. — Milk Sauce for Fish. — Apple Sauce. — Baked Pears. — Stewed Prunes. — Coddled Apples. — Cranberry Sauce.

TENTH LESSON.

Omelets. — Quaker Omelet. — Oyster Stew. — Oyster Soup. — Scalloped Oysters. — Fried Oysters. — Broiled Oysters. — Macaroni Boiled. — Milk Toast. — Baked Custard. — Steamed Custard 112

CONTENTS.

ELEVENTH LESSON.

SICK-ROOM COOKERY 116
Beef Tea. — Sack Posset. — Chicken Broth. — Oatmeal Gruel. — Indian Meal Gruel. — Plum Porridge. Corn Tea. — Wine Whey. — Vinegar Whey. — Sour Milk Whey.

TWELFTH LESSON.

SICK-ROOM COOKERY. — (*Continued.*) 121
Beefsteak. — Mutton or Lamb Chop. — Cream Toast. — Rice Coffee. — Flour Gruel. — Custard. — Eggnog. — A Good Drink for the Lungs. — Other Drinks. — Lemonade. — Cure for Hoarseness. — Burns. — Unfailing Cure for Constipation.

MISCELLANEOUS ARTICLES.

REMARKS ON DIGESTION 125

ADDITIONAL RECEIPTS.

Soups and Stews. — Pea Soup. — Bean Soup. — Onion Soup. — Shin of Beef Soup. — Vegetable Soup. — Clam Soup. — Clam Chowder. — Salt Fish Chowder. — Potato Chowder. — Chicken Chowder. — Tomato Chowder. — Parsnip Stew with Dumplings. — Barley Stew. — Irish Stew. — Mutton Stew. — Corned Beef Stew. — Sausage Stew. — Veal Stew. — Fish Stew. — Vegetable Stew. — Stewed Beef. — Braised Beefsteak. — Veal Pot Pie. — Fricassee of Veal, with Biscuit. — Fricassee of Cold Meat, with Baked Dumplings. — Rolled Flank of Beef. — Beef's Heart. — Sheep's Hearts. — Kidneys. — Baked Liver. — Fried Liver. — Boiled Fish. — Fried Fish. — Broiled Fish. — Salt Fish in Cream. — Salt Fish with Pork. — Macaroni Pie. — Warming Cold Meats. — Cottager's Pie. — Warming Cold Fish. — Cold Pota-

CONTENTS.

toes. — Vegetable Hash. — Cold Vegetables. — Steamed Rice. — Dinner Apple Sauce. — Rhubarb Sauce. — Brown Betty Pudding. — Troy Pudding. — Huckleberry Pudding. — Suet Indian Pudding. — Batter Pudding. — Baked Tapioca Pudding. — Boiled Tapioca Pudding. — Oatmeal Pudding. — Hominy Pudding. — Corn-starch Pudding. — Hot Farina Pudding. — Cold Farina Pudding. — Gingerbread Pudding. — Rice and Apple Pudding. — Steamed Fruit Pudding. — Baked Indian Pudding. — Snow Pudding. — Sunday Pudding. — Baked Rice Pudding. — Hasty Pudding. — Blanc-Mange. — Cold Sauce. — Molasses Sauce. — Plain Pie Crust. — Apple Pie. — Rhode Island Pie. — Rhubarb Pie. — Lemon Pie. — Custard Pie. — Squash Pie. — Doughnuts. — Molasses Cookies. — Plain Sugar Cookies. — Suet Cake. — Spice Cake. — Poverty Cake. — Spice Bread. — Swedish Bread. — Pancakes. — Spider Corn-Cake. — Biscuit. — Steamed Indian Bread 130

INDEX 173

FIRST PRINCIPLES
OF
HOUSEHOLD MANAGEMENT.

CHAPTER I.

THE AIR WE BREATHE.

1. THE earth is surrounded by an atmosphere of air, the height of which is about forty-five miles. We could not live a moment without this air, for we take it into our bodies with every breath we draw. It is a mixture of several kinds of gases, four of which are necessary to its composition.

2. Two of the four elements form nearly its entire bulk; these are oxygen and nitrogen, one fifth being oxygen and nearly four fifths nitrogen. The other two elements are carbonic acid and watery vapor.

3. Oxygen comprises one fifth of the air, three fourths of all animal bodies, eight ninths of the water and about one half of the crust of the earth.

4. It has neither taste nor smell, but it keeps the air pure and healthy, and is the chief supporter of animal life. Fires and lights burn only because of oxygen.

5. After a hall or lecture room has been occupied for any length of time, if the ventilation is not good

the lights will begin to burn dimly, and the people will begin to feel drowsy and oppressed. But if the windows are opened, the pure air filled with oxygen rushes in, and the poisoned air filled with carbonic acid gas rushes out. The people begin to breathe easier and feel better, and the lamps burn brighter.

6. In breathing we take air into our lungs; there the blood absorbs the oxygen and carries it through the body, where it burns up all the waste tissue, and so keeps our bodies warm, strong, and healthy.

7. It is oxygen which makes fruit and vegetables decay, and meat and fish "spoil." For this reason, when we wish to keep any of those things for any length of time, we make them boiling hot, to free them from the oxygen, and then seal them in a jar so tight that no air can enter. If kept perfectly free from this gas they will keep for years.

8. You will ask what is the use of nitrogen in the air? The nitrogen dilutes the air. If the air were undiluted oxygen, animal and vegetable life would burn out too rapidly. "A mixture of the fiery oxygen and the inert nitrogen gives us the golden mean. The oxygen now quietly burns the fuel in our stoves and keeps us warm; combines with the oil in our lamps and gives us light; corrodes our bodies and gives us strength; cleanses the air and keeps it fresh and invigorating; sweetens foul water and makes it wholesome; works all around us and within us a constant miracle, yet with such delicacy and quietness we never perceive or think of it until we see it with the eye of science." (Steele.)

9. **Carbonic Acid.** — Carbonic acid, like oxygen

and nitrogen, is without color, but it has a slight odor and a sour taste. By mixing two parts cream of tartar and one of soda, and wetting them, you can obtain carbonic acid. When soda is added to vinegar, sour milk, lemon juice, or any liquid acid, carbonic acid is produced.

10. When bread is risen by yeast, carbonic acid is produced.

11. It is carbonic acid which gives soda water its peculiar taste, and also causes it to foam.

12. Carbonic acid is a poison to animals if they breathe in much of it, but it is the food of plant life, just the same as oxygen is the food of animal life, and vegetation could no more live without it than we could without the oxygen. This is one of the reasons why people are so much healthier in the country than they are in the city. The leaves of plants which are constantly in the sunlight and are their lungs, breathe in carbonic acid and breathe out oxygen. Thus, we see, vegetation is in great part fed with a gas which is poisonous to animal life. We are breathing in oxygen and breathing out carbonic acid all the time.

13. **Watery Vapor.** — By watery vapor is meant the steam, whether visible or not, which rises from the surface of water when exposed to the air.

14. If it were not for this vapor, vegetation would dry up, and animal life would soon perish also.

15. Besides the vapor which comes from water, there is the animal vapor which we throw out from our lungs and the pores of the skin. This is very impure, and causes much disease.

16. Now that we know what the great bulk of the

air is composed of, and what is good for vegetation and what for animal life, we want to know how we can have pure air at all times.

17. When we are out-of-doors we nearly always have pure air, except it be in very crowded streets; so in the houses where we work and mostly live we must consider ventilation, or letting out the bad air and letting in the good air.

CHAPTER II.

THE HOUSE WE LIVE IN.

1. When possible, the house we live in should have the sunshine on every side of it some part of the day. Trees should not be so near as to shade it from the sun. Windows should open from top and bottom. On the top of a hill it is much more healthy than at the sides or bottom.

2. If there is a cellar under the house, great care must be taken that it is well ventilated, and kept perfectly clean and free from all decaying vegetation. If the house is built without a cellar, it should be raised from the ground at least two or three feet, that a current of air may pass freely under. This is the general mode of building in southern countries. In cold, northern climates a cellar is necessary, both to keep the house warm, and that there shall be a place to keep vegetables and fruit from freezing during the winter months.

3. There should be a supply of fresh air coming through a window or open fire-place in every room *all* the time, *night* and *day*. This is the only way by which the air in a room can be kept perfectly pure.

4. A full-grown person takes about one pound of air into his lungs every hour, so it would not take long to use up all the pure air in a room without ven-

tilation, as in a room twelve feet square and eight feet high the air will weigh but ninety pounds! Besides, every time a breath is taken and the oxygen breathed, carbonic acid is also thrown off; animal vapors, too, from lungs and skin make the air impure. The fire burning in a close stove, the lamp or gas burning, all use up the oxygen.

5. In the summer, during the day, there is little trouble about ventilation, because it is pleasant to have windows and doors open. But at night there are people who sleep with closed windows because they don't like to breathe night air, just as if they could breathe anything else at night. After a person becomes accustomed to sleeping with open windows, there is never danger of taking cold, winter or summer.

6. One safe way, where persons are very sensitive to cold, is to have a board the exact width of the window, and about three or four inches deep; raise the lower sash and place this under it, and there will be an upward current of air which will be sufficient to purify the room, while no draught will be felt.

7. Every morning open the windows of the sleeping rooms, strip the beds, spreading the clothes over the chairs, and let them air at least an hour. There is no greater purifier than the sun. Bed-clothes and mattresses should be well sunned at least once a week.

8. In the kitchen, where cooking and other work is being done, the window should always be dropped from the top. Where wash-bowls are set in sleeping rooms, great care should be taken that the waste-pipe

is kept closed when not being used, as poisonous gases often enter a room in that way, brought from the sewers, causing many diseases.

9. A bed that has been made up a week or more is not fit to sleep in, as moisture gathers, which often proves fatal to persons sleeping in one.

10. If carpets are used on the floors, far better is it that the colors should fade from letting the sunlight in upon them, than the bright hues remain with the sunshine shut out. Remember, always, that the sunshine is one of God's best gifts to use, and that it is sinful to shut it out of our houses for the sake of a carpet or curtains.

11. Flowers brighten, cheer, refine, and make our homes healthful; they grow particularly well in the kitchen, where the heat is even and the air moist from the steam, and here the sun is seldom shut out.

CHAPTER III.

THE WATER WE USE.

1. THE water we use is of as great importance as the air we breathe. It forms three fourths of the surface of the earth, and about three fourths the weight of living animals and vegetables.

2. Pure water is composed of oxygen and hydrogen, eight ninths of its weight being oxygen, and one ninth hydrogen. Hydrogen, like oxygen, has, when a pure gas, neither color, taste, nor smell.

3. In the waters of our wells and rivers there are also vegetable, animal, and mineral substances, beside the gases of the air. The animal and vegetable substances are considered unhealthy by nearly all chemists and physicians, but there is a great difference of opinion in regard to the mineral. The gases from the air give the water a bright, pleasant taste.

4. The purest water we have is rain water collected in the country; after a shower has cleared the air and washed off the roofs of the houses, it is run into cisterns, where sometimes it is filtered. The cisterns should always be exposed to pure air, as the air not only gives flavor to the water, but oxygen, which purifies it by burning up all decaying animal and vegetable matter. Cisterns are divided into two parts; the one where the water first enters being divided from

the other by a filter, which is made of iron, sponge, charcoal, and sand, purifying the water for use.

5. In large towns and cities we do not have wells, because there would not be water enough for all the people, and also the water would be very bad, causing all kinds of dreadful diseases.

6. There are water companies who bring water through pipes from rivers and lakes in the country into reservoirs in towns and cities. In the reservoirs it is strained or filtered, and exposed to the air ; and if it is located on a high hill, when it is let into pipes it will run to the upper stories of houses not higher than the reservoir.

7. It is the wells and cisterns in the country that we want to know most about, as we have no control of the water used in large towns or cities.

8. **Well Water.** — We dig a deep hole in the ground and it fills with water. In some places we must dig very deep indeed before we reach water, which makes the well cost much money. But it is better to pay a good deal of money for a deep well where the water is pure, than to pay doctors for trying to cure us of sickness caused by drinking water from a shallow well which gathers impurities from the soil.

9. Where does the water that flows into the wells come from? You will answer, Out of the earth. Yes, but how does it get into the earth? You will notice that when there has been no rain for a long time the water in the wells gets very low, and some wells grow entirely dry. The wells that dry first are always the shallow ones, and the last ones are the deep ones. Thus we see that the rain waters the earth, and filters

into the wells. It is just like pouring a liquid which we wish to make clear into a sieve. ·If the sieve is coarse, the liquid is not perfectly clear; if we keep on pouring it through one sieve after another, and each sieve be finer than the last, we will soon have it nearly pure ; if there is anything dissolved in it, of course that will go through the finest sieve. Now the deeper the well the purer the water, because the earth is like the sieves, which keep back all the undissolved impurities. In light sandy soils the water filters through very rapidly, and carries with it much impure matter. If the well is near the house, and there are soap-suds or slops, etc., thrown on the ground near it, the rain will carry those impure washings through the earth into the well water. Water from a well so situated is like slow poison, causing many diseases, the most common being fevers. Many people sicken and die from drinking it. Thoughtless people often do their washing near their well, throwing the dirty water upon the ground; or they have no sink-drain, so all the waste water is thrown out of doors and windows, to be finally washed into their well, keeping it poisonous all the time, while they wonder what makes so much sickness in their family.

10. We can see that the rain that falls within a few feet of the well would not be enough to keep the well full of water, but that it must come from some distance, so manure heaps should be at a great distance to prevent them from rendering the well foul.

11. Another source of poisoning is the leaves which fall into the water and decay in the well. It is best

to build a roof over the top, keeping it open at the sides for the air to enter, while the leaves are kept from blowing in. If what I have said about wells will make plain to thousands of people who are daily drinking poisoned water the necessity of keeping the well pure, that they may keep their health, I shall feel well repaid for the labor of writing this little book.

12. Many people living in the country are not rich enough to have a good system of drainage, and many can have none at all. To these the trees and plants do good service, vegetation using for its food what would otherwise serve to poison animal life.

13. A good plan is to have a large tub or barrel placed on a strong wheelbarrow and set in a convenient place where the sun does not shine, and throw into this all slops, which can be easily carried to grove or orchard for watering the trees, and enriching the soil.

14. Remember that you are poisoning people slowly, but as surely, every time you throw dirty water near a well, as if you deliberately put arsenic into it.

15. The usual criterion of pure water is that it shall be "perfectly free from color, taste, or smell; be cool, soft, bright, well aerated, and entirely free from all deposit." This standard is a good general one, but will not always hold true.

16. The city of Savannah, Georgia, is supplied from the Savannah River, which flows through a great deal of yellow clay country, and the water, as we found it on the hotel tables, retained its muddy, dark appearance. The water that you get at hotels

and restaurants in Paris, France, is perfectly clear, bright, and pleasant to the taste, but people fear to drink it. Where there is any doubt of the purity of the water, it is always safest to boil it before drinking, because this destroys the vegetable and animal life it may contain; and if it holds mineral matter, boiling causes that to fall to the bottom of the vessel, allowing the pure water to be poured off. But in boiling you lose the gases, so the water is tasteless and flat.

17. **Hard and Soft Water.** — Soft water is considered by many as the most healthful. Tea and coffee made with soft water are much stronger and better flavored. Vegetables and meats boil more quickly and are more tender when boiled in soft water. Clothes wash more easily and are whiter, needing less soap and labor to cleanse them, when using soft water.

18. In using water for washing, cleansing, cooking, therefore, soft water is the best. Some physicians and chemists claim that hard water is very unhealthy, while others think that persons drinking it have stronger muscles. The French authorities supply the city of Paris with hard water, preferring it to soft, because they found that more conscripts from the soft-water districts are rejected for lack of muscle than from the hard-water districts.

19. Water that has minerals dissolved in it, however, affects different people differently. The water filtering through the earth dissolves some of the minerals over which it flows, the most common of which are lime, salt, magnesia. Where there is a great deal

of lime in the water it curdles the soap, produces a fur on the kettles, and clings to the clothes boiling in it, giving them a dark, dingy look.

20. Washing soda and borax are used to soften the water for washing and cleansing, when too hard.

CHAPTER IV.

HOUSE WORK.

1. WE know now that to be perfectly healthy our houses must be kept entirely clean, and have plenty of fresh air and sunlight. The first thing in the morning, then, is to open the windows wide in the sleeping rooms, and take all the clothes from the beds, spreading them upon chairs, where the air can pass through them freely and carry off the impurities which were thrown out from the body through the pores of the skin during the night. The bed and bedding should be aired not less than one hour.

2. While the rooms are being purified by fresh air, the breakfast should be prepared, the table set, the kitchen and sitting-room put in order.

3. First build your kitchen fire, brush off and blacken the stove or range; then sweep the floor and dust the room. Rinse out the tea-kettle, fill with fresh water, and put upon the stove. Set the breakfast plates into the heater. Take out the ashes and sift them.

4. Now set the table, while the breakfast is being cooked. Have everything clean, hot, and on time.

5. After breakfast, wash the dishes in clean hot soap and water, first washing the glass, which wipe perfectly dry with a clean soft towel; then the silver,

next the cups, saucers, pitchers; then the plates and other china dishes. All but the glass and silver ware should be rinsed in clean hot water. As soon as the dishes are finished and put away, wash the cooking dishes, being as careful to have clean water and towels for them, as for the china, and washing, rinsing, and wiping them as carefully. The tins and iron pans should be wiped with a dry towel, and then put on the hearth to dry perfectly, as they rust very easily and quickly. Pots, kettles, and fry pans should be put into the pan of hot water, and the outsides should be washed as carefully as the insides. Unless the water is very hard, there is no need of putting soda into the water for cleaning kitchen dishes, any more than for glass or silver. The wire dish-cloth helps wonderfully in cleaning cooking dishes, and does not scratch them. Using very coarse sand to scour with scratches the tin off in places, and then the dishes soon begin to rust. Wood ashes, for this reason, is better than sand, and sapolio, a soap which comes for cleaning, is better than either.

6. The dish towels should be washed and thoroughly rinsed every day, and when it is possible dried in the open air. The habit of drying the dish-water into the towel is a very filthy one. On wash days, a new set of towels should be taken for the week, and those that have been used should have a thorough washing and scalding. Let them, if possible, remain on the line over night.

7. When steel knives are used, they should be cleaned after every meal; first by washing perfectly clean, then by placing on a board perfectly flat and

rubbing with fine Bristol brick dust wet with water, applied with a large cork, until the blades are perfectly bright. Now wash again in clean warm water, and wipe dry. The handles of the knives should never be put into the water.

8. When all the dishes are washed, every part of the sink should be thoroughly washed with plenty of hot water and soap with a cloth kept for that purpose; then rinse with hot water. So necessary for cleanliness is hot water, that a good housekeeper should keep the kettle or tank always well filled, that it may be ready for use.

9. **Rule for Keeping Hot Water.** — Every time you take water from the kettle fill with cold.

10. Now the dishes are all washed and put away, and everything is clean in the kitchen, the dining-room must be swept, dusted, and put in order. As soon as breakfast was over, the windows of this room should have been opened to air while the kitchen work was being done. After sweeping it, leave the dust time to settle, while the chamber work is being done.

11. **Chamber Work.** — The first thing to do after turning the mattresses and making the bed is to empty the slops, and with clean hot water wash out the glasses, pitchers, and bowls, and then the slop pans. Have separate cloths for the bowls, pitchers, etc., and the slop jars, and never use the toilet towels for this purpose. Now dust the room, put things in place, and, if in summer, close the blinds, and the room is finished.

12. Except upon sweeping days, which should be once a week, this is about the usual work for a sleep-

ing-room. All the rooms and halls should be dusted every day. Such rooms as are used by many people during the day should be thoroughly swept each morning.

13. The dining-room must next be dusted and closed. The reason why the dishes must be washed and the kitchen put in order first is that they wash more easily than if the food has time to harden on them, so time and labor are saved. Then if dishes and food are allowed to stand upon the tables they collect flies, and food left in the hot kitchen dries or spoils. This order of doing the work gives the beds time to air and the rooms to be purified.

14. **To wash Floors and Tables.** — All wood has what is called the "grain of the wood." It runs up and down the board, and not across it. To wash plain wood work, then, you must rub the cloth or brush up and down the board, not across. Too much soap makes white pine boards yellow. Have clean, coarse cloths, perfectly free from grease, and plenty of hot suds; also a scrubbing-brush. First wash the table with a cloth, then dip the brush into the hot suds and rub with the grain of the wood; when you have thoroughly scrubbed it, wash off with the cloth, wiping off all the soapy water, then wash off with clean hot water, and wipe very dry. Wash white floors in the same manner. Floors should be washed only on bright days. Bedroom floors should be washed early in the day, as it is very dangerous to sleep in a damp room.

15. The cellar must be looked after every few days that nothing be left to decay or spoil there. Much

sickness comes from cellars that are not well aired, and where old vegetables are allowed to decay. No poison in the air is more deadly than that from decaying vegetation. In the autumn many fevers arise from the poisoned air caused by the dying plants and falling leaves.

WASHING.

1. The first days of the week are always best for washing, because the clothing is then washed nearly as soon as changed, and so more easily, as the dirt does not have time to harden in them. Also, because dirty clothes are very unhealthy to have in the house; and, again, it is the time set apart for this work in nearly all families, and therefore people are less liable to interrupt on "wash-day;" lastly, it is best to have the work planned for each day, and then it will be sure to get done in time.

2. For washing you must have plenty of water and soap, and if the water is hard add a little washing soda or borax.

3. Look the clothes over carefully, putting the cleanest by themselves to be washed first. Have two tubs, which about half fill with warm water in which has been dissolved soap enough to make a good suds (hard water will take more than soft). Into one tub put the cleanest articles, having the most soiled at the bottom; into the other tub put the rest of the clothes, always remembering to have the most soiled at the bottom of the tub. Have a third tub of soap suds, hot as you can bear your hands in it. Shake all the dust and lint out of the flannels, putting the cleanest white ones into the hot suds, and wash very carefully,

squeezing and washing them through the water again and again. When clean put them into a pail of clear hot water and rinse very thoroughly. Wring dry, shake out well, and hang in the sun to dry. Flannels washed in this way will not shrink or harden. When nearly dry they should be taken in, folded carefully, and rolled up in a damp cloth so that they shall iron smoothly.

4. For the white clothes, half fill the tub in which the flannels had been rubbed with clean warm water. Now begin with the cleanest articles and wash them carefully; wring them out and put into the tub of warm water; rinse out of this, and put soap on the most soiled parts, which in under-clothes are the bands, sleeves, and waists. Place all in the boiler, with cold water enough to cover them, and let them come to a boil; then take them up and put them in a tub of clean cold water, rinse them thoroughly in this water, then rinse again in warm water which has been slightly blued, wring very dry from this, and hang out. Before being taken from the lines they should be entirely dry. Wash all of the clothes in this manner, having a basket full ready as fast as each boiler full is scalded. Boiling does not improve the clothes. If there are fruit stains on the table-cloths or napkins, lay the stained part over a bowl and pour boiling water through the stain until it disappears. Ink stains will nearly always come out if the article washed is rubbed out in cold water while the stain is fresh.

5. Never use soap on any stain first. Machine oil is taken out of cloth by rubbing a little lard or butter on the spot, and washing in warm water with a little soap.

6. **Iron Rust.** — Spread the garment in the sun, and cover the iron spot thickly with salt; then wet with juice of lemon. If the sun is bright, the stain will disappear in a few hours.

7. To wash lace or curtains that will bear but little rubbing, take one table-spoonful of borax to two gallons of warm water, and soap enough to make a strong suds. Soak the curtains in this over night, and in the morning add a little hot water, washing them very carefully with the hands. Next put them in another tub of strong, warm, clean suds, and wash out of that in the same manner. If after rubbing the water looks very dark, they will need to be rubbed through still another tub of warm suds. Then scald and rinse as you would other white clothes. Remember that curtains are full of dust and smoke, — so need to have a great deal of water used to cleanse them, but very gentle rubbing. There are less fibres in lace to take up the starch, so it must be dried before starching, unlike cotton or linen articles, and the starch must be boiled thick, being quite hot when used. Never iron lace curtains. Place a mattress in a clean spot which is exposed to the sun; on this pin firmly and smoothly a sheet; then upon this pin your curtain, being particular to have the sides all straight, and the whole perfectly smooth to dry in shape. You can dry two curtains at a time very well on one mattress, and, if the sun is bright and warm, they will dry in one or two hours.

8. **Starching and Ironing.** — Starch is made in two ways, raw and boiled. Mix four table-spoonfuls of starch with half a pint of cold water, for raw starch,

which, used on collars, cuffs, and shirt-bosoms, will make them very stiff, they being dry when dipped into the starch. Wet them thoroughly, clap between the hands, and then roll up tight in a clean cloth, and in an hour they can be ironed.

9. For a dress, you would use about eight times as much water. In using raw starch, care must be taken that no part of the garment becomes dry before being ironed, as that would prevent there being any stiffness.

10. Boiled starch is made by mixing raw starch with enough cold water to make a thin mixture, — a cup of water to three fourths of starch, — and then pouring boiling water on it till it becomes the thickness you require, stirring all the time you are pouring the water. If for collars and cuffs, it must be quite thick; the articles should be well clapped between the hands, as that spreads the starch evenly through all the threads of the linen. Dry them, and then dampen in cold water, rolling them up in a cloth. They will iron better if they remain thus for ten or twelve hours. Many of the best laundresses add a teaspoonful of butter or lard to every quart of starch. For colored clothing the starch should be thin and cool, the articles being put into it from the rinse-tub. Articles starched with boiled starch must always be dried and sprinkled before ironing.

11. The ironing-sheet must be quite clean, or it will soil the clean clothes, and the irons should be washed once a month, while warm, in warmer water, in which a little lard is melted; this will keep them clean and smooth. They are hot enough to use when a drop of

water will make them hiss. The clothes should be sprinkled and folded the night before being ironed, and, if carefully and smoothly folded, will iron more easily and quickly.

12. If the starch clings to the iron when passing over the starched garments, place upon a board sand or brick-dust, and rub your iron up and down until the starch is rubbed off.

13. Always try your iron on a piece of paper or cloth before putting it upon a garment, to insure its being clean and not too hot. If it is too hot, set where it will cool, but never throw cold water upon an iron, as that makes it very rough.

14. The ironed clothes should hang in a warm, dry room, airing at least twenty-four hours before being folded and put away, as it is quite dangerous to wear clothing or sleep in sheets not thoroughly aired. Persons often are made very ill by carelessness in this particular.

FIRES.

1. Stoves and ranges are now made so that the ashes and cinders can be taken out without making a dust. First gather all the ashes and cinders from the top of the stove into the grate; then put on the covers, shut the doors, and dump the contents of grate into the ash-pan. Take out the ash-pan and empty into the sifter, return the pan to its place, and close the door. Now put shavings or paper into the grate, and place on top several pieces of light wood, crossing each other so there shall be a draft of air through them. Now add three or four sticks of hard wood and set the shavings on fire, opening all the drafts of

the stove. As soon as the wood begins to take fire, cover about six inches thick with fresh coal. Watch the fire now, that the coal does not burn up too red; but just as soon as it has begun to take fire shut up all the oven dampers, keeping open only the slide in front of the grate.

2. Never have the coal come above the lining of the stove. It is a waste of fuel, and the fire will not be so bright and clear because the draft will not be so good. When you are not using the fire, keep the dampers closed; it will be ready when you need it; then open the drafts. For cooking either on top of the stove or in the oven, no matter how hot the fire desired, having the coal come nearly to the top of the lining, the fire ought to last four hours without new coal or poking. If after dinner you wish to have a good clear fire to bake, let the fire burn quite low, then take off all the covers, and with a long poker rake the coals from one end of the grate to the other. When you have raked down all the ashes in this way, and separated all the coal, put in two sticks of hard wood, fill up with fresh coal, and the fire will be quite as good as if you had dumped the old one. When you just wish to keep enough fire to make tea and toast, put on cinders after dinner, and shut all the dampers until twenty minutes before again needed, when opening the dampers will rekindle it.

3. Some chimneys draw better than others, so that the time it takes for kindling a fire cannot always be told.

4. Fires in open stoves and grates are made in the same way, only a blower is fastened on in front of the

grate until the fire burns brightly; after removing the blower the fire will continue, if undisturbed, for from six to twelve hours.

LAMPS.

1. There used to be a great many kinds of oils burned, and of course a great many kinds of lamps suited to the different oils, but now kerosene oil is what nearly every one uses who has not gas in the house. The wick should touch the bottom of a lamp and be trimmed square across.

2. Keep every part of the lamp perfectly clean, or the air cannot circulate freely and the lamp will not burn well. Never burn a lamp when the oil is very low, as a gas collects in the lamp, which is liable to explode.

3. Do not fill the lamp to the very top, as the heat expands the oil, which forces its way out of the lamp, making it both dirty and dangerous.

4. When you light a lamp, do not turn the wick up much at first, until the chimney is gradually heated, because the inside of the glass heats first, and if the heat is strong at first the glass expands too rapidly and breaks.

5. When you take a lamp from a warm room into a cold one, or into a draft, you must first turn down the wick that the chimney may cool a little; a cold current of air striking on a hot chimney will break it as quickly as heating too rapidly.

6. In a very moist climate, like East Florida, or on the sea-shore, the lamp-chimneys break very often; for cool moist air cools glass more quickly than cool dry air does.

7. When using a lamp to light a room, be sure the wick is turned up high enough to burn freely; if not, the room will soon be poisoned with the gas from it.

8. In case of sickness, where there must be a light kept, if you are without a night lamp, place the common lamp in another room or hall, rather than turn the wick too low.

9. To have a bright fire, or a clear blaze from your lamp, it must be remembered that plenty of fresh air is necessary; the lamp must therefore be kept clean, and the stove free from cinders and ashes.

CHAPTER V.

THE HUMAN BODY.

1. THE human body has often been compared to the steam-engine, and no better illustration can be found. In the engine we have a material structure; in the body we have a material structure also, only very much more complicated. The fuel and water with which the engine is fed answers to the food for the supply of the human body. The same agent, air, is used to consume the fuel in both. The burning of the fuel is necessary in both, that work may be done; and the greater the amount of work to be done, the greater must be the supply of fuel.

ANALOGIES OF
THE STEAM-ENGINE AND THE LIVING BODY.

The steam-engine, in action, takes: —	The animal body, in life, takes: —
1. Fuel. Coal and wood, both combustible.	1. Food. Vegetables and flesh, both combustible.
2. Water, for evaporation.	2. Water for circulation.
3. Air, for combustion.	3. Air, for respiration.
And produces: —	And produces: —
4. A steady boiling heat of 212°, by quick combustion.	4. A steady animal heat, by slow combustion, of 98°.
5. Smoke loaded with carbonic acid and watery vapor.	5. Expired breath, loaded with carbonic acid and watery vapor.

THE HUMAN BODY. 27

STEAM-ENGINE.	LIVING BODY.
6. Incombustible ashes.	6. Incombustible animal refuse.
7. Motive force of simple alternate push and pull in the piston, which, acting through wheels, bands, and levers, does work of endless variety.	7. Motive force of simple alternate contraction and relaxation in the muscles, which, acting through joints, tendons, and levers, does work of endless variety.
8. A deficiency of fuel, water, or air disturbs, then stops, the motion.	8. A deficiency of food, drink, or air, first disturbs, then stops, the motion and the life."

Youmans.

An engine having the speed of sixty miles an hour will consume more fuel and water than one having the speed of only thirty miles an hour; so a person working hard with body and mind will require more food than a person who does but little work. There is a great difference in people as to the amount of food necessary for them, so that it is impossible to lay down a rule showing how much food every person would require.

COMPOSITION OF THE HUMAN BODY.

In a person weighing 154 lbs., the compounds are as follows:—

	LBS.	OZ.	GRS
1. Water, which is found in every part of the body, and amounts to	109	0	0
2. Fibrine and like substances found in the blood and forming the chief solid materials of the flesh	15	10	0
3 Phosphate of lime, chiefly in bones and teeth, but in all the liquids and tissue . . .	8	12	0
4. Fat, a mixture of three chemical compounds, and distributed all through the body . .	4	8	0

		LBS.	OZ.	GRS.
5.	Ossein, the organic framework of bones; chief constituent of connective tissue. Boiled yields gelatine	4	7	350
6.	Keratine, which forms the greater part of the hair, nails, skin, and is a nitrogenous substance, weighs	4	2	0
7.	Cartilagin resembles the ossein of bone, is a nitrogenous substance, and chief constituent of cartilage; weighs	1	8	0
8.	Hæmoglobin gives the red color to blood, and contains iron, is a nitrogenous substance; weighs	1	8	0
9.	Albumen is a soluble nitrogenous substance found in the blood, chyle, muscle, lymph; weighs	1	1	0
10	Carbonate of lime, found mostly in the bone, and weighs	1	0	350
11.	Hephalin is found in nerves, brain, with cerebrin, mugelin, and several other compounds; weighs	0	13	0
12.	Fluoride of calcium is found chiefly in teeth and bones; weighs	0	7	175
13.	Phosphate of magnesia is found chiefly in teeth and bones; weighs	0	7	0
14.	Chloride of sodium, or common salt, is found in all parts of the body; weighs	0	7	0
15.	Cholesterin, glycogen, and inosite are compounds containing hydrogen, oxygen, and carbon; found in muscle, liver, and brain; weigh	0	3	0
16.	Sulphate, phosphate, orgarme, salts of sodium, found in all tissues and liquids; weigh	0	2	107
17.	Sulphate, phosphate, chloride of potassium, are found in all tissues and liquids; weigh	0	1	300
18.	Silica, found in hair, skin, bone, weighs	0	0	30

ELEMENTS OF THE HUMAN BODY.

	LBS.	OZ.	GRS
1. Oxygen, a gas, and supporter of combustion, weighs	103	2	335
2. Carbon, a solid, found nearly pure in charcoal. Carbon in the body is combined with other elements and produces carbonic acid gas, and sets free heat by its burning; weighs	18	11	150
3. Hydrogen, a gas: it is a necessary part of all bone, blood, and muscle; weighs	4	14	0
4. Phosphorus, a solid, found in brain, bones, weighs	1	12	25
5. Sulphur, a solid, found in all parts of the body, weighs	0	8	0
6. Chlorine, a gas, found in all parts of the body, weighs	0	4	150
7. Fluorine, supposed to be a gas, is found united with calcium in teeth and bones; weighs	0	3	300
8. Silicon, a solid, found united with oxygen in the hair, skin, bile, bones, blood, saliva; weighs	0	0	14
9. Magnesium, a metal found in union with phosphoric acid in the bones, weighs	0	2	250
10. Potassium, a metal, the basis of potash, is found as phosphate and chloride; weighs	0	3	340
11. Sodium, a metal, basis of soda, weighs	0	3	217
12. Calcium, a metal, basis of lime, found mostly in teeth, bones, weighs	3	13	190
13. Iron, a metal found everywhere in the body, and is essential to the coloring of the blood	0	0	65

Manganese and Copper Metals. — Faint traces of both these metals are found in the blood and brain.

| 14. Nitrogen, a gas, which is a part of all muscle, blood, and bone; weighs | 4 | 14 | 0 |

By this table you will see there are sixteen elements in the human body, and we must have food every day in which all these elements are. We do not take food into the body in the form of elements, except the oxygen, a great part of which we take in the free, uncombined state. This, however, we have found is not so much a food as an agent to burn the food. Now that we know the elements and compounds of the body, we want a simple table which shall tell us what forms our daily food.

CHAPTER VI.

PHYSIOLOGICAL AND CHEMICAL CLASSIFICATION OF FOOD.

Nitrogen compounds are the chief muscular flesh formers. They may yield fat, and, by their oxidation or burning, set free heat and motion.

Carbon compounds are sugar, starch, etc. They produce heat. The carbon and nitrogen compounds are all combustible, that is, they will burn or oxidize in the body.

Water and mineral compounds, such as phosphate of lime and salt, are not combustible, but they are necessary to the building up and repairing of the body.

The flesh-forming foods are sometimes termed the nitrogenous foods, and sometimes albuminoids.

The foods that produce heat are often termed warmth-giving, and sometimes carbonaceous foods.

We must remember that the nitrogenous foods form muscular flesh, and that the carbonaceous foods produce heat; also that one is as necessary as the other to a healthy body. In winter and a cold climate we require more fat and starch to keep the body warm than we do in a hot climate or in summer. Also, we must have a proper supply of such food as goes to build up the bones and muscles.

ALBUMINOUS MATTERS.

1. Albuminous matters are derived from both animal and vegetable sources, but they are more abundant in animal substances, for which reason animal food is richer and more nutritious than vegetable food, and less of it is needed to supply the waste of the body. Albumen is the principal ingredient in the white of the egg. It is found in the blood, and it is this element which makes it grow hard when exposed to the air or heat. Caseine is the albuminous substance of milk, gluten of flour, and is a common ingredient of all vegetable juices. It exists in two states: one soluble in water, the other insoluble.

2. One of the properties of albumen is that of coagulation, that is, hardening. They do not all coagulate by the same method. The white of an egg will harden when heated to the boiling point; the fibrine of the blood coagulates when exposed to the air.

3. Milk will not coagulate when boiled; but if a piece of rennet is added to it, in a few minutes it will harden if it is blood-warm. This property of coagulation belongs entirely to albuminous substances. Another property belonging to them is that they will ferment. This is also a very important property. When milk or soup has become sour, it has fermented; when we put bread to rise with yeast, it begins to ferment; but if the yeast is sweet and the bread does not rise too long, the bread will be sweet.

4. Fermentation will not take place in a very cold or very hot atmosphere, and will be most rapid about 100 degrees Fahrenheit, that is, about as warm as the human body.

5. Albuminous matters are the only ones that putrefy. All substances containing albuminous matter will, when exposed to the air and moisture, become putrefied, and, if it is warm, much more rapidly than in a cold atmosphere.

6. Animal substances do not putrefy at a very high or a very low temperature, that is, if they are kept at the freezing point or boiling. When we say anything is at a low temperature we mean very cold, and when at a high temperature, it is very hot. So when meat or fish are to be kept for some days we either put them on ice, in a chest, or cook them.

7. If there is no moisture, putrefaction will not take place; for this reason meats and fish are often dried in the air and sun, and they will keep for years if kept in a cool, dry place.

MEAT.

1. We will first consider meat, as it contains the most albuminous matter. If we take a piece of lean meat and strip it up very fine, and then wash it in a number of clean waters, rubbing the meat at the same time, we shall wash away all the soluble part, and there will remain only white threads. These threads are the fibres of the flesh, and the substance of which these threads are composed is named fibrine. It is an albuminous article of food. Fibrine also exists in the blood of animals. Heat, when as great as that of boiling water, hardens and shrinks fibrine, but if the heat is less than boiling and is continued a long time, it softens it.

2. Tough pieces of meat are made very tender by stewing a long time, but they must never boil.

3. When the meat has been thoroughly washed to get the fibrine, the albumen is dissolved in the water. This is a very important part of the meat. It dissolves in cold water, but hardens in hot water. If we put a piece of fresh meat in a pan of boiling water, and another piece in one of cold water, and let them cook the same length of time, we shall find that the water in which the meat was put cold is much richer with the juices of the meat than that which was hot when the meat was put in, and that the meat is poorer in flavor and juices than the piece placed in hot water

4. We see why this is. The hot water coagulates the albumen which is on the surface of the meat; this fills up every little pore, and the juices cannot flow out. But the cold water dissolves the albumen, and draws it all out of the meat. Now if we wish to keep the juices in a boiled piece of meat we must first plunge it into boiling water, and let it boil rapidly for fifteen minutes, to harden the albumen on the outside; then we must set it back where the heat will not be so great, and let it just simmer until done, because we have found that if we boil it the fibres will grow hard and shrivel up. If we wish to make soups, and get all the juices into the broth, we put the meat in cold water and let it heat slowly. We must remember this in broiling and roasting also, — always to have a quick fire for broiling, and when the meat is first put before the fire, or in the oven for roasting, because we first wish to harden the albumen, so that the juices shall not flow out of the meat while cooking,

CLASSIFICATION OF FOOD. 35

To stick a fork into a piece of meat while cooking makes great holes through which the juices flow out and are lost. Nearly all parts of an animal are good for food, the muscular flesh being the best.

5. Stewing is the most economical mode of cooking meats, as then all parts are tender and eatable.

6. Broiling and roasting are the most healthful; next, stewing or boiling.

7. Fried meats cannot be healthful, but are much used, because a very convenient way to cook, and it serves to make variety in the mode of serving meats.

8. All red meats should be cooked rare, and all white meats should be well done. Beef, to be good, must either be cooked very rare, or be thoroughly done.

9. The heart and livers of nearly all animals are very nutritious, but are hard to digest.

10. Tripe is both nutritious and digestible.

11. The tendons and gristly parts can be boiled to a jelly. They consist of a substance called gelatine. The shanks of beef and veal are much used for soups, for the sake of the jelly which they make, and which will keep for a week or more in a cool place.

12. **Salt Meats.** — Salting meats, as in the case of beef and mutton, is very wasteful. The salt extracts the juices, and the brine receives the most nutritious part of the meat. In the case of pork, it makes but little difference, as the fat is not injured by the salting.

MILK.

1. Milk is a naturally prepared food. It contains all the elements of which the body is composed. A

very large proportion of milk consists of water; the cream is largely fat. When milk becomes sour, the solid part separates from the whey, and is called curd. The curd is the albuminous part of the milk, while the cream is the carbonaceous part. The whey left after the curd is taken from the milk contains salt and other mineral matter necessary for digestion, and the earthy matter of which the teeth and bones are formed.

EGGS.

1. Eggs, like milk, contain all the material necessary for the growth of the body. They are composed of two distinct substances, — the yolk and the white. The white consists of water, albumen, and mineral ingredients. The yolk contains nearly a third of its weight in oil, a large quantity of albumen, a very large part of sulphur, and other mineral matters. The sulphur gives the yolk its yellow color, and it is this which causes the eggs to tarnish silver. Eggs are not easily digested by every person, but are very nutritious food for those who can eat them.

2. The most healthful modes of cooking eggs are boiling, poaching, and in omelets. The common mode of putting the eggs into boiling water and letting them boil rapidly for three or more minutes is not the best, as the heat hardens the albumen near the shell; and in this way, while the white of the egg becomes very hard, the yolk has not begun to cook.

3. The better way is to pour boiling water on the eggs, cover them closely, and let them stand where they will keep hot, but not boil, for ten minutes. Then they will be cooked through evenly, — the white and yolk alike.

4. When they are to be cooked hard, they should boil twenty minutes, which is necessary to make them mealy and digestible.

POACHED OR DROPPED EGGS.

5. When eggs are broken into a cup, and then turned gently into a pan of salted boiling water and cooked for about one minute, they are called dropped or poached eggs. They are healthful and inviting cooked in this manner and served on toasted bread.

6. Omelets are prepared by beating the eggs well, seasoning with salt, pepper, and a little milk, cooked in a very hot frypan. There must not be too much of the mixture poured in at once, and the pan should be moved quickly while the omelet is being cooked. This is a very healthful and convenient dish.

7. Eggs are used for custards, puddings, pies, and cakes. They make these dishes lighter and more nutritious. When eggs are beaten very rapidly, they quickly break up into cells filled with air. The white of the egg will retain more air than the yolk, and for this reason it is very useful in making cake, or any other kinds of food where lightness is desirable.

CHAPTER VII.

FISH.

1. Fish is a very healthy and digestible food, but not nearly so nutritious as meat. White fish are much more easily digested than dark, having so much less oil. Fish is very nitrogenous, for which reason a good deal of starchy food should be eaten with it. Potatoes are particularly suitable on this account to be eaten with fish. It is now thought that fish is a better brain food than meat, because it contains so much phosphates.

2. Oysters, clams, and mussels are made indigestible by much cooking. They are all improved by being kept in salted water and meal for a day or two.

3. Lobsters and crabs are not easily digested. Cayenne pepper should always be used in seasoning them, as that helps digestion.

4. Fish must always be thoroughly cooked, and if boiled it should be plunged into boiling water, well salted; then the kettle set back where it will simmer gently until done. Much of the nutritious part of the fish is lost in boiling. If the water is salted, it not only seasons the fish but hardens the water, and thus less of the nutritious qualities are lost.

5. Baking fish carefully renders it one of the most

savory dishes we have, and less of the nutritious qualities are lost.

6. In stewing, or making fish-chowder, all the nutrition is kept.

7. **Frying.** — Nearly all varieties of white fish are fried, which is a very convenient and savory method of cooking, but not nearly so healthful as either boiling, baking, or broiling. The fish should be wiped dry, seasoned with salt and pepper, and dipped into flour, meal, bread or cracker crumbs, and then dropped into boiling fat. There should always be enough fat to cover the fish, and the smoke should rise from the centre of it before the fish is put into it.

8. Salting fish, like salting meat, extracts the juices and hardens the fibres. Fat fish, like fat meats, are not injured to the same extent as white fish. There is a fish that is found in the great lakes named white fish, but all the light fish, such as cod, haddock, etc., are called white fish, because the oil is contained in the liver; while in blue-fish, mackerel, salmon, etc., the oil is found in all parts of the body.

LOBSTERS AND SALTED COD-FISH.

9. Lobsters should be plunged into boiling water while yet alive, and boiled until the shell turns red. They are eaten with a dressing and as a salad, without further cooking, and they are also cooked again in many different ways.

10. A great mistake is often made in cooking salt cod-fish. When it is soaked to extract the salt, it should be placed in a pan of cold water. The skin of the fish being up, the salt will fall on the skin if the

fish is placed with the skin under, and so the fish does not freshen. In the morning, the fish should be placed in the same position and covered with water, and then let come to a boil; cover tightly, set back where it will not boil, and cook for five or six hours. Fish cooked in this manner will be tender and juicy. Boiling hardens the fibres of the salt-fish just the same as it does meat. Salt-fish cooked in this way, and served with potatoes, beets, carrots, and salt fried pork or butter sauce, makes a very substantial dinner. What remains from dinner can be used for a great many dishes, such as hash and fish-balls. All cold fish left from one meal can be warmed up in some way to be a savory dish and used again.

CHAPTER VIII.

VEGETABLES.

1. A certain amount of fresh vegetables is necessary to perfect health. The most common and useful with us are the potato, squash, turnip, beet, cabbage, and onion, because they can be kept for many months after being gathered from the garden.

2. **The potato** is the most general in use. Three fourths of the weight of the potato consists of water; the greater part of what remains is starch, with a little fibrine, albumen, and small quantities of mineral and other matters. Being so largely composed of starch classes it among the carbonaceous foods.

3. **Turnips.** — Nine tenths of the weight of the turnip consists of water. It contains no starch, but has mineral, pectose, and other matters in small quantities. Some chemists think that it is a nutritious food, and others think that there is very little nutriment in it. Having so much pectose and no starch, it is a good vegetable to be eaten with potatoes.

4. **Squash.** — A large proportion of the squash is water, while starch, sugar, albumen, and mineral matters are found in it. As a food it is pleasant and healthful.

5. **Beets.** — The beet is also largely water; has

sugar, minerals, albumen, and three parts pectose. It belongs to carbonaceous foods.

6. **Cabbage** is now considered by some chemists to be one of the most nutritious vegetables. It is composed of about nine tenths water, and the remainder albumen, starch, sugar, gum, fat, mineral, and other matters. With potatoes, rice, or any starchy food, cabbage, or any kind of greens, is very valuable as food.

7. **Onions** are used for flavoring soups and stews, and by many persons they are eaten both raw and cooked. There is a great difference in strength of smell and flavor in the different kinds of onions, those grown in our northern climates being much stronger than those from a southern climate. The onion is used not only in cookery, but often in sickness. It contains no starch, and belongs to the nitrogenous or flesh-forming class of foods.

8. **Sweet Potatoes.** — The sweet potato belongs to the carbonaceous class of foods, as so large a part of it consists of starch and sugar. Seven tenths of its weight is water.

9. **Tomatoes.** — Nearly nine tenths of the tomato consists of water. The next largest substance is sugar. It contains no starch, but albumen, malic acid, cellulose, pectose, and mineral matters. It is four times more warmth-giving than flesh-forming.

10. All fresh green vegetables when well cooked are very healthful.

Pease and Beans. — When green, pease and beans are very nutritious and easily digested. When dried, they are still a very nutritious food, but are not so digestible. When dried, they require a great deal of cooking. They are very nearly alike in composition : over one half is starch, one fourth casein ; the remainder is water, mineral matters, etc. The casein resembles the curd in cheese, and belongs to the flesh-forming or nitrogenous foods, so that these vegetables by themselves form a more perfect food than any other of which we have spoken. If a small teaspoonful of mustard be added in the cooking of beans, there is less danger of their producing colic, as they often do when eaten by some persons.

Carrots and Parsnips. — Carrots and parsnips are somewhat alike in their composition. The parsnip contains albumen, sugar, starch, cellulose, lignose, pectose, dextrine, fat, and mineral matter. The carrot contains albumen, sugar, cellulose, lignose, gum, pectose, fat, and mineral matter. There is no starch in carrots, but more sugar, so that its heating power equals the parsnip.

SALADS.

1. Under salads are classed all green vegetables that are eaten uncooked. This term is now commonly applied to all vegetables, meats, and fish which are eaten with a dressing made of oil, vinegar, salt, etc. In this place we shall only speak of the vegetable. Those most used as salads are lettuce, celery, cress, sorrel, chicory, tomatoes, and cucumbers ; also some kinds of cabbage.

2. Nearly all the food value that lettuce contains is in the water and mineral matter which it introduces into the body, but it is a very refreshing dish when eaten with rich food.

3. **Celery.** — Celery is much richer in nutrients. It is three times as great a heat-giver as flesh-former. It is used as a salad, as a seasoning for soups, and, when cooked, as a vegetable.

4. **Water-cress.** — This salad is grown in wet places and shallow-running streams. It has nearly the same food value that celery has. It is always eaten uncooked. Great care must be taken in washing and preparing these salads, as there are frequently little insects upon them.

5. **Cucumbers.** — Cucumbers have but little food value, and to some persons are very injurious. They are eaten when uncooked as salads, and are also cooked in various ways.

CHAPTER IX.

FRUITS.

FRESH fruits are very necessary to perfect health. They must be ripe and sound to be entirely healthful. Unripe and decaying fruit causes a great amount of sickness and death every year in our large cities, where it is sold at low prices on the streets. The most useful of the fruits, and very extensively grown, is the apple. It is not only good eaten fresh, but it can also be cooked in more ways than any other fruit.

Figs, dates, and bananas, either fresh or preserved, are very healthful, nutritious fruits.

CHAPTER X.

THE BREAD WE EAT.

1. THE bread we eat is made from wheat, rye, Indian corn, and sometimes oats and rice.

2. Wheat is the principal grain used for bread. There are a great many kinds of wheat, more than one hundred and fifty!

3. The red wheat, from which macaroni and vermicelli are made, contains a greater amount of nitrogenous substances than the white wheat does. It is harder, and is not so floury.

4. Wheat is composed of nearly two thirds starch, about eleven parts albuminoids, water, mineral, and other matters. Whole wheat meal, on an average, contains one part flesh-formers to six and a half of heat-givers.

5. In different kinds of flour the amount of starch varies. There are now two processes of making flour: one is called the old process, or St. Louis flour, and the other the new, or Haxall flour. In the new there is more starch and less of the albuminoids, the flour makes a very handsome white bread, which keeps moist for a long time, from the fact that starch in baking is changed to gum. It is questionable if this is the best flour to build up the body.

6. Wheat and all cereal grains consist of three layers of bran-coats and the inside or heart of the grain. The outer coat of the grain has but little food value, and as it is very hard and irritating to the digestive organs it is better to have it removed from the wheat before grinding.

7. The greater part of the gluten, phosphates, etc., are in the bran-coats. The inside of the grain consists of cells filled with starch. When the wheat is ground by the old process, a great part of this bran is ground so fine that after being sifted many times some of the bran still remains. This makes the flour darker, but also much more healthful and nutritious. The less of the bran-coatings there is in flour the whiter it is.

8. Graham meal, or, as it is now commonly called, whole wheat meal, is the whole wheat ground rather fine and not sifted. But we do not always get the pure wheat meal. It is oftener a poor quality of flour with which common bran has been mixed.

A great difference of opinion exists concerning which is the more nutritious, flour or Graham; some scientific persons claiming that flour is robbed of its most healthful parts, while others claim Graham is not so nutritious as flour for hard-working people, because in its irritation of the digestive organs it causes the digesting fluids to flow more freely, and so hastens the food through the various channels too rapidly, not allowing time for proper digestion or absorption. Both of these theories are right in part, but to a hard-working person we would advise the use of flour as the most nutritious and economical of the two, because all of it is digested.

For persons of quiet habits, such as students and persons in offices or stores, the Graham would be better.

9. If you will take a little flour and wet it with cold water, enough to make a dough, and then place it on a sieve and pour a stream of cold water over it, working the dough all the time with one hand until the water that runs through the dough is no longer white, you will have remaining on the sieve the gluten of the flour; and after the water has stood a while, at the bottom of the pan there will be pure wheat starch, which you can get by pouring off the water very carefully. The water that you have poured off from the starch contains the sugar, gum, and mineral matter; these being dissolved in the water, they cannot be separated like the gluten and the starch.

By washing a little dough in cold water we have learned some very important things. That the gluten of the flour does not dissolve in cold water; that it is of a rather grayish color; that it is tough and elastic, something like India rubber. This tough, elastic property is very important in bread and pastry making.

10. When bread is made with yeast, the yeast uniting with the sugar of the flour produces carbonic acid gas. This gas tries to escape from the dough, but the tough gluten makes a wall which holds it back. The gas goes on forming in the dough, and soon there is a panful of light sponge where a few hours before there was about a third of a pan of solid dough.

Next, we learned that the starch of the flour does not dissolve in cold water; and if we pour off the

THE BREAD WE EAT. 49

water and let it dry, we shall find it is composed of grains which, if rubbed between the hands, will give off a crackling sound, and be fine and powdery. If we could examine these grains with a glass, we should find that each grain is covered with an outer skin, that will not dissolve in cold water; but if we put the starch in boiling water these skins crack, and the insides are then dissolved and become gummy. We see from this how important it is that everything into which starch enters should be thoroughly cooked.

INDIAN CORN.

11. Indian corn is poorer than wheat as a flesh-former, but richer than rice. It contains more fat than any of the other grains except oats. It is used in this country in a great many forms as food. It is eaten, while green, from the cob, as a vegetable; the whole pearled grains as samp; the broken grains as hominy; and the ground grains as meal; and in a very fine powder it is sold as corn starch, but it is rarely used as a laundry starch. In any form it makes a healthful addition to our food, but it is particularly convenient and palatable in the form of hominy or meal. The hominy is ground from quite fine to very coarse. The meal, also, is ground coarse and fine. There are two processes for grinding meal. The old one gives a very sweet-flavored meal when it is first ground, but owing to the heating that it gets between the millstones and the moisture in the corn, it will grow musty very quickly. The product of the new process, called granulated meal, keeps perfectly well for years in all climates. The corn is first dried for

two years or more, and then ground by a process which gives coarse grains like granulated sugar. In using this kind of meal, more wetting must be used than with the old-process meal. In New England the yellow corn meal is the most used, but in the Southern and Middle States the white corn meal is much more used.

OATMEAL.

Oatmeal is richer in flesh-formers than wheat flour. It is used as a mush, eaten with milk, cream, butter, sugar, or syrup, the most common being sugar and milk. It is prepared for the market in different ways, one of the best being pearled oatmeal; that is, all the hard outer husks are taken off, and it is then crushed slightly. It is also ground very coarse, medium coarse, and very fine. For most persons, oatmeal is very healthful; but there are persons with very delicate stomachs who should not eat it unless it is very thoroughly pearled: the husks irritate the lining of the stomach. Oatmeal, as indeed all other meals, should be very thoroughly cooked.

Stir it into plenty of boiling water, and boil two hours. Bread is sometimes made of fine oatmeal, but not very often in this country.

RYE.

Rye meal and flour are more used in New England than in any other part of the country. It is used in the form of bread and mush. The flour is often made into raised bread; the meal is used in brown bread and muffins and third bread. Rye meal is a healthful addition to the bread materials by giving variety and coarseness to our breads.

RICE.

Rice is sometimes used in the form of flour in bread and cake making, and sometimes the whole rice is first boiled and then added to flour or meal in making bread. But the most common mode is to use it as a vegetable, or in puddings.

Rice contains a great deal of starch, a small quantity of fibrine, no fat, a very little mineral and other matter. It is not by itself a nutritious substance, but when used with milk and eggs is good and healthful food. Also, when used as a vegetable with meats it takes the place of potatoes.

PEARLED BARLEY.

Barley is mostly used in soups; but it is sometimes ground into flour and used with wheat flour for bread making. It is not as nutritious as wheat, but in soups it is a very delicious thickening. It requires a great deal of boiling, — never should be boiled less than two hours.

BUCKWHEAT.

Buckwheat is richer in nitrogenous substances and has less starch than wheat, so that it is a greater flesh-former than wheat. The common mode of using it in this country is in the form of griddle-cakes. The amount of starch and fat contained in the buckwheat renders it very heating. It causes a slight eruption on the face of many persons after they have been eating it a few weeks.

BREAD MAKING.

Americans have more kinds of bread than any other nation, but they do not always have better, and generally not as good, bread as is found in other countries. As bread is one of the articles which we eat at every meal, it is one of the most important in the whole list of foods, and should be studied as carefully as possible.

Good bread, to be healthful, must be light, porous, nd perfectly sweet. There are a great many ways of making bread.

1st. By mixing with yeast.

2d. By using leaven.

3d. By salt-risings or milk yeast.

4th. By mixing the flour with water which is highly charged with carbonic acid. This is called aerated bread.

5th. By baking powders, or soda and cream of tartar.

6th. With cold water, and a great deal of beating.

Yeast bread is by far the most healthful and economical of all the modes of making bread. There are a great many rules for making yeast bread, but the first principles are always the same. These are one quart of flour, a little more than one fourth of a quart of water, one fourth of a cup of liquid yeast or one fourth of a cake of compressed yeast, one fourth of a table-spoonful of salt, one fourth of a table-spoonful of sugar. The water should always be blood-warm, and the dough thoroughly kneaded to distribute the yeast evenly through it, and also to render the grain of the bread fine and uniform. Milk is often used instead of water, and generally a little butter or lard is added to the dough to make the bread more tender. Bread with these ingredients must of course be more nutritious than that made with water; but there is no bread that has the delicious sweet taste of the wheat, and that will keep as long, as yeast bread made with water. As the bread depends so much upon the yeast, great care must be taken that it is quite sweet and fresh. The compressed yeast made by Gaff, Fleischmann & Co., when fresh, will always make good bread. This firm have done a vast amount of good in this country by the introduction of their yeast and the examples they give us of what good bread is. If all our bakeries could copy their bread, there would be a great change in the comfort and healthfulness to bread-buyers. When the dough is mixed, the water softens the gluten, and causes all the particles of flour to be cemented together. The yeast causes fermentation, changing the sugar of the flour and the sugar added to the flour into carbonic acid and alcohol: it also changes part of the starch into sugar. Carbonic acid gas being very light, it seeks to escape and mix with the air, but here it cannot do so because of the gluten.

HOW BREAD CHANGES IN THE BAKING.

The bread in baking loses about one sixth of its weight, but the loaf grows larger while baking, because the heat expands the carbonic acid, turns the water into steam and the alcohol into vapor. These escape through the pores of the bread, so that after baking and cooling neither carbonic acid nor alcohol is left in the bread. Baking also changes a great part of the starch into gum. Some of the starch belonging to the wheat does not change, except that the cells are broken and the starch dissolved so that it is digestible. The gluten becomes tender, and unites with the starch paste.

LEAVEN.

Leaven is a paste made with flour and water and allowed to sour. Sometimes housekeepers and bakers keep a piece of the risen dough for the next bread mixing, and they call this leaven. In many of the bakeries of Paris they do this, and use a little dry yeast with it in making common bread, but it always gives to the bread a slightly sour taste.

SALT-RISING BREAD.

In salt-rising a batter is made with flour, salt, milk, and water a little more than blood-warm. The basin in which the batter is must be covered and placed in another basin of blood-warm water, and kept in a warm place near the fire, where it will keep at that temperature until it becomes a perfect sponge; more flour is then added to it, and all is well kneaded and put in the baking-pans, and allowed to rise again till ready to bake. Bread made by this process is very sweet and delicate, but one tires of it very quickly.

AERATED BREAD

Aerated bread is made by mixing the flour with water into which carbonic acid has been forced under high pressure. As soon as the pressure is removed the bread begins to rise, and is baked immediately.

BAKING POWDERS.

Soda and cream of tartar and baking powders are used to make unfermented bread. Baking powders are a composition of an acid and an alkali. The acid takes the place of cream of tartar, and the alkali of soda; in fact, it is nearly always bicarbonate of soda. Baking powders, when pure, are the most convenient and safest mode of using chemicals where the cook is without a perfect knowledge of the relations between soda and cream of tartar; because, to be perfectly harmless, they must each neutralize the other. It takes three fourths of cream of tartar to neutralize one fourth soda, if both articles are pure. It is a great mistake to mix the cream of tartar with the flour and then dissolve the soda with water, because you then must use a little more soda than would be necessary if you mixed the dry flour, soda, and cream of tartar together.

Bread made with cold water is usually in the form of gems. The water must be very cold, the oven very hot, and the gem-pans hot. The water and salt are added to the Graham or wheat flour, and the batter is beaten very rapidly and thoroughly. This is to mix air with the batter. The mixture is then dropped by the spoonful into the pans, and they are immediately put into the oven and baked. In another chapter we shall have more exact rules for bread making.

CHAPTER XI.

THE CONDIMENTS, SPICES, AND FLAVORS WE USE.

CONDIMENTS.

Of the condiments we use, salt and pepper and mustard are the most important.

Salt, taken with foods, undergoes certain changes in the body. Its chlorine helps to supply the hydrochloric acid of the gastric juice. Sodium forms part of the soda salts, which are the elements of the bile. Salt is very necessary to the health of both human beings and the higher animals. Only one race of people is known that does not use salt in food. A traveler found a tribe of people in Central Africa that did not use salt, and they did not seem to suffer from the loss of it. Civilized people, if deprived of salt for any length of time, become sick. Salt is used in nearly every dish that is cooked, and also in preserving meats and fish. Salt should be fine, dry, and white, and without a bitter taste. In boiling vegetables in soft water, when salt is added it slightly hardens the water, and so preserves the color and juices of the vegetables, besides giving them a better flavor.

Pepper. — There are three kinds of pepper, —

black, white, and red. The black pepper is found in the market both whole and ground. The whole pepper is called pepper-corn. These pepper-corns are ground, and we then have black pepper.

White pepper is made from these black pepper-corns, also, but the outer shells, or covering, are first removed before grinding. This gives it a different flavor and much lighter appearance than the black.

Cayenne, a red pepper, consists of pods, or seed vessels, of different species of capsicum, ground to a powder. Though not so much used in cookery as black pepper, it is far more healthful, the red being stimulating, while the black is irritating. Cayenne is often used as a medicine : taken as a hot drink for colic or colds, used as a gargle with vinegar for sore throats, and sometimes with hot vinegar to bind on the throat when sore.

Mustard. — Mustard is used as a condiment and often as a medicine, great quantities being used in malarial countries for pastes and mustard baths. It is made from the seeds of both black and white mustard, which are first crushed between rollers, and then pounded in mortars. When used with food the powder is simply mixed with water; thus it is taken with cold meats. It is also employed to season some dishes while they are being cooked. When taken in small quantities it is good for digestion, but if in large quantities it proves very injurious, as it irritates the lining of the stomach.

Among other condiments which we use are mint, thyme, parsley, sage, sweet marjoram, and summer **savory**. The leaves of these are used either green or dried for soups, sauces, and meats. When used carefully they add to the healthfulness of the food by making it more palatable.

SPICE.

Spices are usually added to articles of food containing sugar, and sometimes to meats and soups. The most common of these are ginger, nutmeg, cinnamon, clove, mace, and allspice. We get all these spices in the market for cooking purposes in three forms, whole spice, ground spice, and extracts. The ground spice is the most convenient and common mode of using them. A very little spice in an article of food will give it a pleasant taste. Where there is much used it hides the natural flavors of the food and spoils the appetite for simple food, beside causing irritation in the stomach. The habit which school-girls have of eating cloves and cinnamon is a very injurious one, and often lays the foundation for ill health in after years, if it does not have immediate bad effects.

Ginger is the most healthful of all the spices, and is much used in sickness, the same as mustard is. The spices are frequently mixed together in seasoning cake, pies, soups, and meats. The great art, then, is to be able to season so that one spice may not be tasted more than another. It will be easy to mix them with the following table, — beginning with the strongest and ending with the mildest. Ginger is seldom used in this mixture: 1. Cloves; 2. Mace; 3. Nutmegs; 4. Allspice; 5. Cinnamon. If we begin with cloves, we increase the quantity of each spice, until reaching cinnamon, we shall take four times as much as of the cloves. This is not the place to speak of the herbs, but this is true of them also. Sage is the strongest, and you should not use more than half as much of it as of the other herbs. Both in spices and herbs a mixture of all kinds is very much nicer than a large quantity of only one.

FLAVORS.

In the market we have the extracts of nearly every kind of fruit for flavoring in cookery. Sometimes the extracts are not taken from the fruit at all, but are artificial essences. The most common, and the ones that we are surer are taken from the fruit, nuts, or berries from which they are named, are lemon, orange, vanilla, and bitter almond. Lemon and vanilla are more used than any other of the flavors. It is always cheapest, safest, and best to buy in large bottles, and that made by manufacturers who have a reputation to maintain. Very small quantities of the pure extracts are healthful, because they make the food more palatable; but there is nothing used in cookery where more care is necessary that there should not be too much used. An article while hot should never be seasoned with an extract if it is possible to add it after it cools, as the heat wastes the strength of the flavor, and more must of course be used. Where an article is to be frozen, three times as much flavoring and sweetening also must be used as when it is to be eaten cold. The usual rule is a teaspoonful of lemon or vanilla to a quart of custard, blancmange, pudding, etc. For sauces twice as much is needed. . Bitter almond and pine apple are both very strong, and when too much of either is used the result is unhealthful and unpleasant. One fifth of a teaspoonful gives a delicate flavor.

The fruits and the vanilla bean are used instead of the extracts. Where the fresh fruit can be had it is much better to use.

A RULE FOR USING CONDIMENTS, SPICES, AND FLAVORINGS.

Use only enough to give the food a delicate flavor.

CHAPTER XII.

TEA, COFFEE, CHOCOLATE, ETC.

TEA.

THERE are three varieties of the tea-plant; both black and green tea can be prepared from them all. Green tea is made from leaves which are dried quickly. Black tea is made from leaves which have first been allowed to stand twelve hours or more before roasting. The leaves wilt and grow moist in that time, and that is what gives the dark and peculiar appearance to this tea. In making tea the pot should be earthen, rinsed with boiling water, and left to stand for a few moments on the stove to dry; then put in the tea-leaves, and let it stand a few minutes longer, and pour on the boiling water, leaving the tea-pot standing where it will be at the boiling point, but not boil, for from three to five minutes. For moderate strength use one teaspoonful of tea to half a pint of water. If the water is soft it should be used as soon as it boils, for boiling causes all the gases which flavor the water to escape. But if the water is hard it is best to boil it from twenty to thirty minutes. The gases escape from hard water also, but boiling causes the mineral matter, which hardens the water, to settle on the bottom of the kettle, and the water becomes softer.

COFFEE.

There are a variety of coffees, but unlike the teas they do not owe their difference of flavor or color to the curing, but to the soil and climate in which they grow. Coffee grows on small trees. The fruit is something like the cherry, but there are two seeds in the fruit. The beans are separated by being bruised with a heavy roller; they are then washed and dried. The longer the raw berry is kept the riper and better flavored it becomes. In countries where coffee is grown, the leaves of the tree are used as much as the berry for making coffee. Like tea, coffee must be roasted that the fine flavor shall be developed. There are large establishments now for roasting and grinding coffee. The work is done by machinery, and nearly always the grains are evenly roasted, and just enough to give the right flavor. If the coffee after roasting is placed in close tin cans, it will retain its best qualities for a long time. It can be ground when needed for use. Many persons think that heating the dry coffee just before making improves the flavor. There are many modes of making coffee, each one having its advantages and disadvantages.

Boiled Coffee. — The old method of boiling coffee is still practiced by at least one half the housekeepers in this country. It is sometimes boiled with an egg, which makes it perfectly clear, and also enriches it. When an egg is not used, a small piece of salt-fish skin is boiled with the coffee, to clear it.

Rule for Boiled Coffee. — One small cup of roasted and ground coffee, one third being Mocha, the other two thirds Java, one small egg-shell, and all broken into the pot with the dry coffee; stir well with a spoon, and then pour on three pints of boiling water. Let it boil from five to ten minutes, beginning to count from the time when it begins to boil. As soon as it has boiled enough pour in one cup of cold water, and turn a little of the coffee into the cup to see that the nozzle of the pot is not filled with coffee grounds; turn this back again, and let stand a few moments to settle. Be sure that it does not boil again. Advantages of the boiled coffee: When the egg is used the yolk gives a very rich flavor, and when the milk or cream is added the coffee has a rich yellow look, which is very pleasing. It also has a peculiar flavor, which many persons prefer to the flavor given by any other process. Disadvantages: The egg coats over the dry coffee, and when the hot water is added the coating becomes hard, and a great deal of the best of the coffee remains in the grounds after the boiling. Also, in boiling much of the fine flavor is lost in the steam that escapes from the pot.

FILTERED COFFEE.

Another, and really the most economical and easiest, way of making coffee is by filtering. The French coffee biggin is very nice for this. It consists of two cylindrical tin vessels, one fitting into the other: the bottom of the upper one is a fine strainer; another coarser strainer, with a rod running from the centre, is placed upon this; then the coffee, which must be very finely ground, is put in, and then another strainer is placed at the top of the rod. The boiling water is now poured on, and the pot set where it will keep hot, but not boil, until the water has gone through. This will make a clear, strong coffee, with a rich, smooth flavor. The advantage of the two extra strainers is that the one coming next to the fine strainer prevents the coffee from filling up its fine holes, and so the coffee is clear, and made with more ease. The upper strainer causes the boiling water to fall on the coffee in a shower, like rain. In this way it is more evenly distributed, and the fine coffee is not carried through the fine strainer, as it would be if the water were poured directly on the dry coffee. When milk or cream is added to this, it does not turn a rich yellow, as in the case of that boiled with an egg. A few spoonfuls of this coffee, without sugar or milk, aken after dinner, is said to help digestion.

STEAMED COFFEE.

Another mode of preparing coffee is steaming it. The coffee is put into the pot, and the boiling water poured on it. This pot, which is made to fit into a tea kettle, is then placed in the kettle, and let cook from ten to twenty minutes, the water in the kettle boiling all the time. This will make a clear, delicious coffee. Some persons think that by first wetting the coffee with cold water and letting it come to a boil, and then adding the boiling water, more of the strength of the coffee is extracted. When there is not cream for coffee, the milk should be boiled, as it makes it much richer. As soon as the milk boils up it should be taken off the stove, since it grows strong and oily by much boiling. To many persons it is in-

TEA, COFFEE, CHOCOLATE, ETC. 65

jurious to drink coffee. Physicians say that if coffee is drunk without milk it is perfectly harmless. Some element in the coffee combines with the milk to form a leathery coating on the stomach, which impairs digestion. A great many substances are mixed with coffee to cheapen it, — chicory, beans, pease, rye, wheat, being the most common; but there are also a number of other things with which coffee is adulterated. To obtain it pure, the safest way is to buy it unground, unless you purchase from a strictly honorable firm. Persons drinking coffee, as a general rule, eat less, though coffee, and also tea, have little direct food value; but they retard the waste of the tissues, and so take the place of food. The sugar and milk used with them give some nutriment.

COCOA.

Cocoa is very rich in nutritious element. Like milk, it has all the substances necessary for the growth and sustenance of the body. It is the fruit of a small tree which grows in Mexico, Central America, the West Indies, and other islands. The fruit is in shape like a large, thick cucumber, and contains from six to thirty beans. There are a number of forms in which it is sold in the market, the most convenient and nutritious being chocolate; next comes cocoa; then cocoa nibs; and last cocoa shells. The beans of the cocoa are roasted in the same manner as coffee, the husks or shells taken off, and it is then ground between hot rollers. Sometimes the husks are not taken off at all, but ground up with the bean. The ground bean is called cocoa, and mixed with sugar, after being ground very fine, is termed chocolate. Vanilla is often added as flavoring. Sometimes the cocoa is mixed with starch. When the bean is broken into small pieces, these are called nibs.

To Make Cocoa. — Put a gill of the broken cocoa in a pot with two quarts of water, and boil gently three hours. There should be a quart of liquid in the pot when it is done; if the pot has boiled so rapidly that there is not this much, add more water, and let it boil once more. This same cocoa will do to be boiled again. Many prefer half broken cocoa and half shells. If the stomach is delicate, it is better than all cocoa. Sugar and milk are used with it, the same as with tea and coffee.

Shells. — Use twice as many shells as broken cocoa, and boil twice as long.

CHOCOLATE.

Scrape one ounce (one of the small squares) of Baker's, or any plain chocolate, fine; add to this two table-spoonfuls of sugar, and put into a small saucepan with one table-spoonful of hot water; stir over a hot fire for a minute or two, until it is perfectly smooth and glossy; then stir it all into a quart of boiling milk, or half milk and half water; mix thoroughly, and serve immediately. If the chocolate is desired richer, take twice as much chocolate, sugar, and water. Made in this way, chocolate is perfectly smooth and free from oily particles. If it is allowed to boil after the chocolate is added to the milk, it becomes oily and loses its fine flavor.

COOKERY.

FIRST LESSON.

BREAD AND YEAST.

Material for the Lesson. — Flour, seven and a half quarts; yeast, one and a half cups; sugar, one small tea-cup; salt, five table-spoonfuls; milk, one pint; Graham, one heaping pint; hops, one heaping table-spoonful; lard, two heaping table-spoonfuls; six large potatoes; time, about three hours.

HOP YEAST.

Material. — Six potatoes; one fourth cup of sugar; three table-spoonfuls of salt; one heaping table-spoonful of hops; half pint of flour; half cup of yeast. Pare the potatoes, and put them in a saucepan with *boiling* water enough to cover them. Let them boil thirty minutes. As soon as you put the potatoes on to boil, put the hops into another saucepan with three pints of cold water; cover the saucepan, and let the hops boil gently until the potatoes are done. Mix the salt, sugar, and sifted flour together. When the potatoes are cooked pour off the water; mash them very light and smooth; then strain the hop water through a fine sieve on the potatoes; stir well, and add the mixture of flour, salt, and sugar; mix all very thoroughly, and strain the mixture through a colander into a stone jar. When it is blood-warm add the yeast; cover tight, and set it to rise where it will be warm. It will rise in five hours. When risen, it will have a thick white froth on top. Now put into a stone jug or into bottles; cork tight, and set on the cellar bottom or in the ice-chest, or, if you have neither, in the coolest place you have. Remember that great heat, like pouring boiling water on it, will kill the plant in the yeast, and also that freezing will do the same thing. The bottles or jug in which the yeast is kept must be washed out first with cold water, and then with soap and water; and after that boiling water must be poured in, and let stand in it for at least half an hour. Yeast often becomes sour from the jug not being properly cleaned before being filled. The cork, too, must have the same care. In hot weather, the yeast should be made once a week. Plan to make enough for the bread, and to have enough to rise the new yeast. In very warm countries the dried yeast is the most used, and it is very convenient for rising liquid yeast in country places where the liquid yeast is not good. It is made by stirring into the fresh yeast Indian meal enough to make it so thick that it can be rolled out into sheets. It is then cut into little squares, placed on boards, and dried in the sun. It takes about three days to dry it.

YEAST BREAD.

Material for Four Loaves of Bread. — Flour, two quarts; salt, half table-spoonful; sugar, half table-spoonful; lard, half table-spoonful; yeast, half cup; water, nearly three fourths of a quart. Sift the flour into the bread pan; take out a cupful of it to use in kneading the bread; then add salt, sugar, yeast, and the water, which must be blood-warm (about one hundred degrees, if in cold weather, and about eighty degrees in hot weather). Beat well with a strong spoon. When well mixed sprinkle a little flour on the board, turn the dough out on this, and knead from twenty to thirty minutes, and put back in the pan. Hold the lard in the hand long enough to be perfectly soft; rub it over the dough; cover close, that neither air nor dust may get in, and set where it is warm. It will rise in eight or nine hours. In the morning shape into loaves or rolls. If loaves, let them rise one hour, where the temperature is between ninety and one hundred; if rolls, let them rise one hour and a half. Bake in an oven that will brown a teaspoonful of flour in five minutes. (The flour used for a test should be put on an old piece of crockery, as it will then have a more even heat.) The loaves will take from forty-five to sixty minutes to bake, and the rolls will bake in thirty if placed close together in the pan; but if French rolls are made, they will bake in fifteen minutes. As soon as baked, the bread should be taken out of the pans, placed on the table, where they can rest against something until they are cool; they should then be put in a stone pot or tin box which

HINTS ON BREAD MAKING.

Kneading. — When you put the bread on the board, mix it lightly. Do not *press down*, but let all your motions be as elastic as possible. Knead with the *palm* of the hand until the dough is a flat cake, and then fold; keep doing this until the dough is light and smooth and will not stick to the board or the hands. Use as little flour as possible in kneading. Do not stop kneading until you have finished. Bread that is " rested " is never so good. Milk can be used instead of water in mixing the bread. It should always be scalded first, and then let cool to blood-heat. One table-spoonful of lard or butter makes the bread a little more tender when water is used.

In cold weather, some kitchens grow cold very quickly after the fire goes out. In that case, the bread should be made earlier in the evening and set in a warmer place (about eighty or ninety degrees); because if it begins to rise well the first two hours, it will continue to rise, unless the temperature of the room falls to the freezing-point. The reason for letting the rolls rise longer than the loaves is that the rolls being smaller, heat penetrates them much more quickly than it does the loaf, and of course fermentation is stopped sooner; therefore the small rolls do not rise so much in the oven as the large loaves. The best sized pan for loaves is made of block tin, eight and a half inches long, four and a half wide, and three deep. Rolls should be made into smooth little balls, and should be placed in even rows in a shallow pan. Breakfast rolls are first made into the little balls, and then rolled between the two hands to make long rolls of about three inches; these are placed close together in even rows in the pan. Dinner or French rolls are first made into little balls, and put on a well-floured board; a little rolling-pin, two and a half inches in circumference, is then well floured and pressed nearly through the centre of the little balls of dough; they are then placed in the pans, but should not touch each other. Being so small and baking so quickly, they have a very sweet taste of the wheat.

The Pans. — The pans for wheat bread should be greased very lightly, either with butter or lard; for rye, Indian, or Graham, they must be greased thoroughly, as the dough clings to the pans more. There are a great many kinds of bread which you can make readily and safely after having learned to make simple, good bread. It is difficult to give exact rules for flour, as it varies so, some flours requiring much more water than others. The new process flour, having so much more starch and packing so much closer than the old process, requires one eighth less flour, or one eighth more liquid; but if it is weighed, it takes the same amount of water for a pound of either process flour. The best flour is always the cheapest for bread making.

There is no one article of food of so great importance, as to the health, comfort, and happiness of the family, as bread. Make it perfect.

GRAHAM BREAD.

Material for Two Loaves, or Twenty-four Muffins.— Water or milk one pint, flour one pint, Graham one *large* pint, sugar half a cup, yeast half a cup, salt one teaspoonful. Have the milk or water blood-warm; add the yeast to it. Have the flour sifted in a deep dish; add yeast and milk gradually to the flour, beating until perfectly smooth; set in a rather cool place (about sixty degrees) to rise over night. In the morning add the salt, sugar, and then the Graham, a little at a time, beating vigorously all the while. When thoroughly beaten, turn into two bread pans, and let it rise an hour, in a temperature between ninety and a hundred. Bake one hour.

Muffins. — Graham muffins are made the same as the bread. Fill tin muffin pans two thirds full, and let them rise to the top of the cups; then bake in a rather quick oven twenty minutes. They will rise in one hour.

To the Teacher. — For this lesson the bread should have been put to rise the night before, also the sponge for the Graham. The first thing in the morning, when the pupils meet, is to shape the risen bread into loaves and rolls, and then put them where they shall be rising; then to add the remainder of the ingredients to the sponge for the Graham, and put that in the pans and muffin cups, making one loaf and twelve muffins. Then have potatoes prepared and put on to boil for the yeast, then the hops, and while they are cooking two batches of bread can be started: one by the teacher, to show how it is done, letting each pupil practice kneading on this batch; then one of the pupils should begin a new batch, the remainder of the class directing her. This dough will answer for an afternoon class, if put where the temperature is between ninety and a hundred; or for a class the next morning, if it stands in the kitchen for an hour, and is then set in a cold room, where it will rise very slowly. The yeast can now be made, and while it is cooling the baking and cleaning up may be done, additional notes given, and dresses changed, so that there shall be no delay, but as soon as the bread is baked the class may be dismissed. The yeast will have cooled meantime, and the half cup of yeast will be added. The pupils knowing all about the temperature and the time, they cannot fail to understand this important element of bread making. The bread lesson is the hardest of all the cooking lessons, on account of the rising; but if these simple directions are followed the foundation will be laid for good bread making all through the after life of the pupil, and nothing should stand in the way of the perfect mastering of this lesson.

When more or all Graham is desired in the bread, the sponge can be made with the Graham, using, however, only half as much yeast: as there is so much more gluten in the whole wheat, it ferments more rapidly than the fine white flour. Demand of each pupil that she make bread and yeast at home, and report to you.

SECOND LESSON.

Material for Lesson. — Two pounds of beef for stew, six pounds of beef for roasting, one pound of beef for broiling, eight potatoes, two slices of carrot, two of turnip, one onion, one and one fourth quarts of flour, one and three fourths quarts of milk, one pint of Graham, five eggs, one large cup of sugar, one table-spoonful of butter or lard, one and one half teaspoons of soda, three teaspoons of cream of tartar or four and a half of baking powder, salt, pepper, flavoring, one pint of stale bread.

BEEF STEW.

Two pounds of beef (the round, flank, or any cheap part; if there is bone in it, two and one half pounds will be required), one onion, two slices of carrot, two of turnip, two potatoes, three table-spoonfuls of flour, salt, pepper, one generous quart of water.

Cut all the fat from the meat, and put in a stewpan and fry gently for ten or fifteen minutes. While the fat is frying cut the meat in small pieces, and season well with salt and pepper, and then sprinkle on two table-spoons of flour. Cut the vegetables into very small pieces, and put them in the pot with the fat; fry them for five minutes, stirring all the time to prevent burning. Now put in the meat, and move it about in the pot until it begins to brown; then add the quart of boiling water. Cover over, let it boil up once, skim, and set back where it will just bubble for two and a half hours; then add the potatoes cut into slices, and one table-spoonful of flour, which mix smooth with half a cup of cold water, pouring about one third of the water on the flour at first, and when perfectly smooth adding the remainder. Taste now to see if the stew is seasoned enough, and if not add more salt and pepper. Let the stew come to a boil again, and cook ten minutes; then add the dumplings. Cover tight, and boil rapidly ten minutes longer.

Mutton, lamb, or veal can be cooked in this same manner. When veal is used, fry out two slices of pork, as there will not be much fat on the meat. Lamb and mutton must have some of the fat put one side; as there is so much on these kinds of meat they are very gross.

DUMPLINGS.

One pint of flour measured before sifting, one half teaspoonful of soda, one of cream of tartar, one half of salt, one of sugar. Put all into a sieve, mix thoroughly, and run through the sieve; then wet with a small cup of milk; sprinkle a little flour on the board, turn the dough (which should have been stirred into a smooth ball with a spoon) on it, roll about half an inch thick, cut into small cakes, and cook ten minutes, as directed. Things to be carefully noted: That the dumplings boil just *ten* minutes; that they do not sink too deep in the soup; that the soup is boiling rapidly when they are put in; that the cover fits tight on the pot, so that the steam shall not escape; and that the pot boils all the time, so that the steam shall be kept up. These few directions carefully followed will insure success every time.

ROAST MEAT.

Put the meat rack into the baking pan; wipe the meat with a wet towel; lay it on the rack; then sprinkle well (on all sides) with salt, pepper, and flour, letting the bottom of the pan get well covered with the flour and seasonings. Now put into a very hot oven for a few minutes, and when the flour begins to become a dark brown turn in hot water enough to cover the bottom of the pan; close the oven door, and let the meat get well browned, but not scorched, on one side; then baste with the gravy from the pan, dredge with flour and brown again. Now turn the meat over, baste with gravy, dredge with salt, pepper, and flour, and brown on this side. A piece of beef weighing six pounds will require forty minutes if it is desired rare, twenty minutes longer if well done. Mutton the same time. Lamb one hour and ten minutes. Veal two and a half hours. Pork three hours. Put the meat on a large hot dish; take the rack from the pan; skim all the fat from the gravy; add half a cup of boiling water, if there is about that amount in the pan; mix one teaspoonful of flour with cold water enough to make a thin paste; stir this into the boiling gravy; season with salt and pepper, if you like it; strain and serve. Remember that you must keep adding water to the pan all the time the meat is roasting, as the bottom of the pan should be covered all the time; and yet if there is too much water in the pan at once it steams the meat. *Never* roast meat without having a rack in the pan, because if the meat is put into the water it becomes soggy, and has no good flavor. Putting salt on fresh meat draws out the juices, and it would not be well to use it if the flour were not used also ; but the flour makes a paste which keeps all the juices in the meat, and also help enrich and brown it; so that by using both salt and flour we get a rich, well-seasoned piece of meat, which we could not by either alone. A very poor piece of meat may be greatly improved by constant basting. Beef requires that it shall be cooked either a very little or a great deal to be good. Between the two extremes it is always hard and indigestible, — unless, of course, the pieces are choice, like the tenderloin and sirloin. The choicest and most expensive parts of the beef are the tenderloin, the sirloin, the five ribs called the fore rib from the fore quarter, and the middle ribs. All the cheap parts of the beef are good for stews and soups, and this is the most economical mode of cooking all meats, as in this way nothing is lost. Two pounds of meat will make a good dinner for a family of six or eight when made into a stew, the same piece of meat not being enough for four if fried or roasted ; besides if the meat is tough it is so much more easily digested when stewed. The cheapest parts of the beef are the neck, the flank, the shin, the heart, and the liver. Good ox beef has a fine grain, yellowish-white fat, and a bright red color. Cow beef has white fat, and the color is a paler red than the ox beef. It is not rich and juicy like ox beef. Mutton and lamb should have the fat white and the meat firm. The meat should be dark. Veal should be firm to the touch, and at least three months old before being killed. The fore quarter of the three last-mentioned meats is always the cheapest. Steaks are cut from the sirloin, the tenderloin, the rump, and the round. The most economical is the round steak, and when the beef is large and tender, and the steak cut from the top of the round, it is a very delicious piece of meat.

BROILING.

For broiling the fire must be clear; coals from a hard-wood fire or charcoal are best, but the most common fires for broiling are the hard coal. Beefsteak should be cut three fourths of an inch thick, sprinkled with salt, pepper, and flour, put in toaster, and placed over the fire; as soon as it begins to brown on one side, which should be in two minutes, turn and brown on the other side; keep turning every few minutes until done, which should be in ten minutes if the steak is to be rare, but fifteen if well done. Now place on a warm dish, butter, and send to the table instantly. Chops are broiled in the same way, omitting the flour. Never use a fork to turn chops or steak, as much of the juices of the meat is lost that way. When there are no coals over which a steak or chop can be broiled, heat the frypan very hot, and put into it about a teaspoonful of butter to prevent the steak from sticking; then put in the steak, and cook about the same time as if broiling over the coals. Fish is broiled in the same way, only that the broiler must have a little pork or butter rubbed over it before the fish is put on. It must, however, broil more slowly than beefsteak or chops, and therefore longer. Halibut is very much improved by standing an hour in melted butter or olive oil before being broiled. All fish that is split must have the inside put to the fire first, and when that begins to look a handsome brown the side on which the skin is should be turned to the fire. Care must be taken that the skin does not scorch, as it does so very readily.

BOILED POTATOES.

Pare the potatoes, and let them stand in cold water an hour or two; then put them on in a kettle, which has a close cover, with boiling water enough to cover them. Let them boil fifteen minutes; then for every twelve potatoes add one table-spoonful of salt, and boil fifteen minutes longer. Now pour off all the water; set the kettle on the back part of the stove, with a clean towel over the potatoes, for three minutes, that they may dry and yet have the steam pass off. Shake them up and turn into a hot dish, and send to the table immediately. It takes them half an hour to boil, five minutes to dry and be served; so that you want to put them on just thirty-five minutes before time for sitting down to the table. No vegetable requires more care in boiling than the potato, and yet none gets less. Remember, the water must be *boiling* when the potatoes go into it, and must boil all the time they are on the fire; that the water must be poured off as soon as they are done; and that they must be served as soon as dry.

GRAHAM MUFFINS.

Materials. — One pint Graham, one pint flour, one pint milk, one half cup of sugar, one teaspoon of salt, one of soda, two of cream of tartar, two eggs.

Put Graham in the mixing bowl. Put flour, sugar, salt, soda, and cream of tartar in the sieve; mix all thoroughly; then pass through sieve into the Graham; mix all well with the hands. Beat the eggs very light in another bowl; add the milk to them; now pour this on the dry ingredients, and beat up well. Have the muffin pans well greased, and put a large table-spoonful of the batter into each cup; bake twenty minutes in a quick oven. This will make twenty-four. Rye and Indian are made in the same manner.

BREAD PUDDING.

Materials. — One pint of stale bread, one quart of sweet milk, one teaspoon of salt, three table-spoons of sugar, two eggs.

Soak bread and milk together for two hours; then mash all up fine with the back of the spoon; beat eggs, sugar, and salt together, and add to the bread and milk; turn into the pudding dish, and bake in a slow oven for forty-five minutes. Run a knife or the handle of a spoon down the centre of the pudding, and if it does not look milky it is done. Serve with cream sauce.

CREAM SAUCE.

One egg, half a cup of powdered sugar, three table-spoonfuls of milk, half a teaspoonful of vanilla or lemon extract.

Beat the white of the egg to a stiff froth; then beat in the sugar, then the yolk of the egg and the flavoring, and last, the milk. Serve immediately, as it spoils by standing.

THIRD LESSON.

Materials for Lesson. — One quart can of tomatoes, four or five pounds of fish, three potatoes, one turnip, one carrot, three onions, one clove, quarter of a pound of pork, two and half quarts of milk, one cup of molasses, three large crackers, two stalks of celery, one egg, six pounds of beef, one pound of liver, four table-spoonfuls of butter, pepper, salt, half a table-spoonful of parsley, three table-spoonfuls of Indian meal.

POT-AU-FEU.

Six pounds of beef, half a pound of liver, one large carrot, one large turnip, one and a half table-spoonfuls of salt, one clove, two onions, one stalk of celery, five quarts of water. Let the beef be any of the cheap pieces. Wipe clean, and put into the soup kettle with four quarts of cold water. Let it come to a boil very slowly, and skim; then add the salt and liver, and set where it will simmer for two hours, every half hour adding one cup of cold water, and as soon as the soup comes to the boiling point skim carefully. After two hours add the clove and vegetables, and simmer two hours longer. Skim off all the fat, turn some of the clear soup into the tureen, and dish the meat and vegetables on a large platter; placing the meat in the centre, and slicing the vegetables and placing them around it for a garnish. There will be soup enough for two days.

BAKED FISH.

Materials. — Any large fresh fish weighing from four to five pounds, three large crackers, quarter of a pound of pork, two table-spoonfuls of salt, quarter of a teaspoonful of pepper, half a table-spoonful of parsley, two table-spoonfuls of flour.

Scrape and wash the fish clean, and rub into it one table-spoonful of salt; roll the crackers fine, and add to them the parsley, half the pepper, half a table-spoonful of salt, a table-spoonful of chopped pork, and an eighth of a cup of water. Put this into the fish, and fasten it together with a skewer. Now cut gashes across the fish, about half an inch deep and two inches long; cut the remainder of the pork into strips and put them in the gashes. Now dredge well with flour. Put a tin sheet in a baking pan, lay the fish on this, cover the bottom of the pan with hot water, put in a rather hot oven, and bake one hour, basting very often with the gravy in the pan, and each time dredging with salt, pepper, and flour. The water must be renewed in the pan very often. When done, lift the fish out of the pan on the tin, and slide it carefully on the platter. Now set the baking pan on top of the stove, and if there is not gravy enough to make half a pint, add more water. Mix one teaspoonful of flour with cold water; stir it into the boiling gravy, season, and serve on the dish with the fish.

TOMATO SOUP.

Materials. — One quart can tomatoes, two heaping table-spoonfuls of flour, one table-spoonful of butter, one teaspoon of salt, one of sugar, one pint of hot water. Let tomatoes and water come to a boil; rub flour, butter, and one spoonful of tomato together; stir into boiling mixture; add seasoning. Boil all together fifteen minutes; rub through a sieve, and serve with toasted bread.

POTATO SOUP.

Materials. — Three potatoes, one pint of milk, half an onion, one stalk of celery, one half table-spoonful of butter, one teaspoon of salt, one eighth of pepper.

Pare potatoes and cover with boiling water; boil thirty minutes. While potatoes are boiling cut up onion and celery, and put on to boil with milk. When potatoes are done drain, and mash light and fine; then turn boiling milk on them; rub through a sieve, and serve *immediately*. This soup spoils if it is let stand, and is not good even when kept hot, but is very delicious if eaten as soon as cooked.

BAKED INDIAN PUDDING.

Materials. — One third cup of Indian meal, one cup of molasses, two and one half table-spoonfuls of butter, two table-spoonfuls of salt, one egg, two quarts of milk.

Let one quart of the milk come to a boil. Pour the *boiling* milk *gradually* on the meal, stirring all the time; when perfectly smooth turn back into the boiler (which must be set into another of boiling water) and cook thirty minutes, stirring often. Now add the molasses, two table-spoonfuls of the butter, the cold milk, the egg, and salt. Butter a deep earthen dish, pour the mixture in, and bake in a moderate oven two and a half hours.

FOURTH LESSON.

Materials. — One pound of cold meat, one and a half pints of cooked salt-fish, two quarts of potatoes, one ounce of pork, four fifths of a cup of flour, three quarts of milk, three cups of Indian meal, three cups of rye, one half a cup of molasses, teaspoonful of soda, salt, pepper, two eggs, one cup of sugar, one table-spoonful of vinegar, fat for frying, two table-spoonfuls of butter, one cup of oatmeal, one cup of hominy.

MEAT HASH.

Chop fine any kind of cold meat (before chopping dredge with salt and pepper. This is always the best manner of seasoning hash, as by this means all parts will be seasoned alike). If you have *cold* potatoes, chop fine and mix with the meat; if they are *hot*, mash. Allow one third meat to two thirds potato. Put this mixture in the frypan with a little water to moisten it, and stir in a spoonful of butter; or, if you have nice beef drippings, use that instead of butter. Heat slowly, stirring often, and when warmed through cover, and let it stand on a moderately hot part of the stove or range twenty minutes. When ready to serve, fold as you would an omelet, and dish. Save all the trimmings and pieces that are left of all kinds of meat, and have a hash once or twice a week. It does not hurt a hash to have different kinds of meat in it. Avoid having a hash (or indeed any other part of your cooking) greasy. It is a great mistake to think that seasoning anything highly with butter improves it ; on the contrary, it often ruins it by disguising the natural flavor, and giving you an unhealthy dish. I have nothing to say against a moderate use of butter in cooking, but I do strongly protest against the immoderate use of it in soups, gravies, hashes, stews, and on meats and fish of all kinds.

FISH BALLS.

Chop very fine half a pint of cooked salt-fish (you will find the rule for cooking salt-fish in the chapter on fish). Boil six good-sized potatoes, and turn them into the tray, with the fish, as soon as they are done ; now mash them light and fine with the potato-masher ; mix thoroughly with the fish ; taste to see if salt enough ; add one table-spoonful of butter, and one egg, if you like, but they will be good without either. Shape into round balls about the size of an egg, and fry in boiling fat until they are a handsome brown. It will take about five minutes. If you like them very moist use one quarter of a cup of milk.

FISH HASH.

One half pint of finely chopped salt-fish, six good-sized cold-boiled potatoes chopped fine, one half cup of milk or water, salt and pepper to taste. Have two ounces of pork cut in thin slices and fried brown; take the pork out of the frypan, and pour some of the gravy over the hash; mix all thoroughly, and then turn into the frypan, even it over with a knife, cover tight, and let it stand where it will brown slowly for half an hour; then fold over, turn out on the platter, and garnish with the salt pork.

OATMEAL MUSH.

Oatmeal, Indian meal, and hominy all require two things to make them perfect: that is, plenty of water when *first* put on to boil, and a *long* time to boil. Have two quarts of boiling water in a saucepan, and stir into it one cup of oatmeal; let it boil one hour; then add a generous half table-spoonful of salt. Boil one hour longer, stirring often.

HOMINY.

Wash in two waters one cup of hominy, stir it into a quart of boiling water, add a table-spoonful of salt, and boil from thirty to sixty minutes. Sixty are better than thirty. Stir often, and be careful that it does not burn. The fine hominy cooks more quickly than the coarse. To be eaten as a vegetable with meat, with butter and sugar, or with milk. It is much more nutritious than rice.

MINUTE PUDDING.

One pint of milk, one of water, nine table-spoonfuls of flour, one teaspoonful of salt, two eggs. Set the milk into a basin of hot water, and when it comes to a boil add to it one pint of boiling water. Have ready the flour, made into a smooth paste with one cup of milk, and mix with this paste, after they are well beaten, the two eggs. Now take the basin in which the milk and water are, and set upon the fire; let it boil up once, and then stir in the thickening; beat it well, that it may be smooth, and cook three minutes longer. Serve with vinegar sauce.

VINEGAR SAUCE.

One cup of boiling water, one of sugar, one table-spoonful of flour, one of vinegar, and a little nutmeg. Mix the flour with a little cold water, and stir into the boiling sugar and water; then stir in the vinegar and nutmeg, and boil twenty minutes. Wine sauce is very good made in this manner, using wine instead of vinegar. Season with a little salt.

BROWN BREAD.

Very nice. Three cups of Indian meal, three of rye, one half of molasses, one table-spoonful of salt, one teaspoonful of saleratus; wet with one and one fourth quarts of milk. Steam five or six hours. This will make enough to fill a two-quart pan.

FIFTH LESSON.

Materials. — Six pounds fish, five potatoes, one large onion, three fourths pound pork, one and one half pounds beef, twelve large apples, one cup molasses, three and one half cups rice, one cup raisins, four and one fourth quarts milk, one table-spoonful cinnamon, one quart flour, four table-spoonfuls butter, two and one fourth cups sugar, six crackers, salt, pepper, one teaspoon cream of tartar, one half soda, flavoring, three eggs.

FISH CHOWDER.

Take either a cod or haddock ; skin it (loosen the skin about the head, and draw it down towards the tail, when it will peel off easily). Then run your knife down the back close to the bone, which you take out. Cut your fish in small pieces and wash in cold water. Put the head and bones on to boil in two quarts of hot water ; have five potatoes pared and sliced thin ; put a layer of potatoes and then one of fish in the kettle ; dredge well with salt, pepper, and flour ; keep putting in alternate layers of potatoes and fish until all is used. Take about one and one half table-spoonfuls of salt in all, one half a teaspoonful of pepper, and one small cup of flour. Fry brown half a pound of salt pork, and then add to it the onion cut in thin slices; fry slowly for ten minutes; now pour all through a strainer, over the fish and potatoes, pressing all the gravy through; then pour on the pork and onions in the strainer one pint of hot water, to get all the goodness out of them. Now strain the water in which the head and bones were boiled into the pot, cover, and let simmer gently ten minutes; then taste to see if seasoned enough; if not add more; and also five crackers. Cover, and simmer ten minutes longer. Serve.

BEEF OLIVES.

One and one half pounds beef, cut very thin. Trim off the edges and the fat; now cut into strips three inches wide and four long; season well with salt and pepper; chop the trimmings and the fat very fine; add to it three table-spoonfuls of powdered cracker, one teaspoonful of sage and savory mixed, one fourth of a teaspoonful of pepper, two teaspoonfuls of salt. Mix all very thoroughly, and spread on the strips of beef; then roll them up, and tie with twine. When all are done roll in flour. Have a quarter of a pound of pork fried brown; take the pork out of the pan and put the olives in; fry brown, then put them in a small saucepan that can be covered tight. Now into the fat remaining in the pan put one table-spoonful of flour, and stir until perfectly smooth and brown; then pour in gradually nearly a pint and a half of boiling water. Stir for two or three minutes, season to taste with pepper and salt, pour over the olives, cover the saucepan, and simmer two hours. Take up and cut the strings with a sharp knife; place them in a row on the dish, and pour the gravy over them.

VEAL OLIVES.

Veal olives are made in the same manner, except that a dressing like chicken dressing is made for them. For one and a half pounds of veal take three crackers, half a table-spoonful of butter, half a teaspoonful of savory, one fourth of sage, one teaspoonful of salt, a very little pepper, and one eighth of a cup of water. Spread the strips with this and proceed as for beef olives.

BOILED RICE PUDDING.

Pick and wash clean one cupful of rice, and put into a basin with a pint and a half of cold water; set on the stove where it will cook slowly, or, better still, set into another basin of water, and cook slowly. When the rice has absorbed all the water, turn on it one quart of new milk, and stir in one table-spoonful of salt; let this cook two hours, stirring often. Serve with sugar and cream.

BOILED RICE PUDDING, NO. 2.

Pick and wash one cup of rice, and boil in one quart of boiling water fifteen minutes, and then drain dry. Wring a pudding-cloth out of boiling water, and spread in a deep dish, and turn the rice into it, and sprinkle in one cup of raisins and a table-spoonful of salt; tie the cloth loosely that the rice may have room to swell, and boil two hours. Serve with lemon sauce, or sugar and cream.

BAKED RICE PUDDING.

Boil half a cup of rice in one pint of water thirty minutes, and then add one quart of new milk, and boil thirty minutes longer; then beat together one cup of sugar, three eggs, two teaspoonfuls of salt, and a little lemon or nutmeg; stir this into the rice and turn the mixture into a buttered pudding-dish, and bake thirty minutes. To be eaten without sauce.

BAKED RICE PUDDING, NO. 2.

Pick and wash one cup of rice; put it into a dish that will hold two quarts or more, mix with it two teaspoonfuls of salt, one table-spoonful of cinnamon, four of sugar, and three pints of milk. Set this in a moderate oven, and stir once in every half hour. After it has been baking two hours, stir in one pint more of milk, and bake one hour longer.

APPLE DOWDY.

Pare and quarter about one dozen good tart apples, put them in a kettle with one cup of molasses, a small piece of butter, and one pint of hot water. Set this on the fire, let it come to a boil, and while it is heating make a paste with one pint of flour, one teaspoonful of cream of tartar, one half of saleratus, and a small cup of milk; roll this large enough to fit into the kettle, and when the mixture begins to boil put the paste in, cover tight, and boil gently twenty minutes. To be eaten without sauce. This is very nice when the apples are tart and it is made well.

LEMON SAUCE.

Beat to a froth one table-spoonful of butter, one cup of sugar, one table-spoonful of corn starch, and two eggs. When very smooth and light add one cup of boiling water. Set the basin into boiling water, and stir five minutes. Season with half a teaspoonful of lemon, and serve.

SIXTH LESSON.

Materials. — Two cups of molasses, one cup of Indian meal, three table-spoonfuls of butter, two quarts of milk, three and a half cups of sugar, one and three fourths quarts of flour, one teaspoonful of ginger, two and a half teaspoonfuls of soda, three teaspoonfuls of cream of tartar, salt, seasoning.

SOFT MOLASSES GINGERBREAD.

One cup of molasses, one teaspoonful of saleratus, one of ginger, one table-spoonful of butter or lard, a pinch of salt, if you use lard. Stir this together, and then pour on one half a cup of boiling water, and stir in one pint of flour. Bake about one inch deep in a sheet. This is very nice if pains are taken to have the water boiling, and to beat it well when the flour is added.

SPONGE–CAKE.

Three eggs, one and a half cups of sugar, two of flour, one half of cold water, one teaspoonful of cream of tartar, one half of saleratus. Beat the sugar and eggs together, and add the water when they are light, then the flour, in which mix the saleratus and cream of tartar. Flavor with lemon, and bake in a quick oven twenty minutes. This will make two sheets of cake.

CREAM PIES.

Make the crust the same as sponge-cake, and bake in four deep tin pans. When cool split in two with a sharp knife, and fill with the cream filling.

FILLING FOR CREAM PIES.

One pint of new milk, one cup of sugar, half a cup of flour, two eggs. Put the basin in which the milk is into another of hot water. Beat the sugar, flour, and eggs together until they are light and smooth, and when the milk boils stir in with one teaspoonful of salt. Cook twenty minutes, stirring often. Flavor with lemon. This will fill four pies. The pint of milk must be generous, and the half cup of flour scant.

WASHINGTON PIES.

Make the crust the same as for cream pies, and fill with any kind of jam or jelly. If you wish, you can make one pan of cake and two pies from this rule.

WHITPOT PUDDING.

One cup of Indian meal, one of molasses, a teaspoonful of salt. Scald thoroughly with one cup of boiling water. Add a quart of milk; pour into the baking-dish and bake one hour, *stirring thoroughly at least twice while it is baking.* Let it get about half cool before you serve it.

VEGETABLES.

It is impossible in a book of this kind to give rules for the cooking of every kind of a vegetable, but we will give some general rules which will cover them all.

Green Vegetables. — All green vegetables must be washed thoroughly in cold water, and then be dropped into water which has been salted and is just beginning to boil. There should be a table-spoonful of salt for every two quarts of water. If the water boils a long time before the vegetables are put in it has lost all its gases, and the mineral ingredients are deposited on the bottom and sides of the kettle, so that the water is flat and tasteless, the vegetables will not look green and have a fine flavor. The time of boiling green vegetables depends very much upon the age, and how long they have been gathered. The younger and more freshly gathered the more quickly they are cooked.

TIME-TABLE FOR COOKING VEGETABLES.

Potatoes, boiled	30 minutes.
" baked	45 minutes.
Sweet potatoes, boiled	45 minutes.
" " baked	60 minutes.
Squash, boiled	25 minutes.
" baked	45 minutes.
Green peas, boiled	20 to 40 minutes.
Shelled beans, boiled	60 minutes.
String beans, boiled	1 to 2 hours.
Green corn	25 to 60 minutes.
Asparagus	15 to 30 minutes.
Spinach	1 to 2 hours.
Tomatoes, fresh	1 hour.
" canned	$\frac{1}{2}$ hour.
Cabbage	$\frac{3}{4}$ to 2 hours.
Cauliflower	1 to 2 hours.
Dandelions	2 to 3 hours.

TIME-TABLE FOR COOKING VEGETABLES.

Beet greens	1 hour.
Onions	1 to 2 hours.
Beets	1 to 5 hours.
Turnips, white	45 to 60 minutes.
" yellow	1½ to 2 hours.
Parsnips	1 to 2 hours.
Carrots	1 to 2 hours.

Nearly all these vegetables are eaten dressed with salt, pepper, and butter, but sometimes a small piece of lean pork is boiled with them, and seasons them sufficiently.

SEVENTH LESSON.

Materials. — Two quarts of beans, one and a half pounds of salt pork, eight potatoes, one beet, one turnip, one carrot, one onion, three eggs, one head of lettuce, four table-spoonfuls of oil, one large cup of vinegar, one cup of milk, one table-spoonful of mustard, salt, pepper, one table-spoonful of molasses.

SALADS.

Salads are quickly and easily made, and can be prepared from almost any of the cold vegetables. We do not give in this lesson (for practice) any of the rich salads, but shall give a few receipts that the pupils may use if the teacher thinks best. In that case the plain salads must be omitted.

FRENCH SALAD DRESSING.

Three table-spoonfuls of oil, one table-spoonful of vinegar, one saltspoonful of salt, one half of pepper. Put the salt and pepper in a cup and then add one table-spoonful of the oil; when all is thoroughly mixed add the remainder of the oil and the vinegar. This is dressing enough for a salad for six persons. If you like the flavor of onion, grate a little of the juice in the dressing.[1]

[1] Onion juice is got by first peeling the onion and then grating

SALADS.

BOILED SALAD DRESSING.

Three eggs, one table-spoonful of oil, one table-spoonful of sugar, one table-spoonful of mustard, scant, one table-spoonful of salt, one teacup of milk, one teacup of vinegar.

Put oil, salt, mustard, and sugar into a bowl, stir until perfectly smooth, then add the eggs, beat well · now add vinegar, then milk ; now place the bowl in a basin of boiling water, and stir until it thickens like soft custard. The time of cooking depends upon the thickness of the bowl. If it is a common white bowl and the water is boiling when it is placed in it and kept boiling all the time, it will take from eight to ten minutes, but if the bowl is very thick it will take from twelve to fifteen minutes. This will keep two weeks if bottled tight and kept in a cool place.

VEGETABLE SALAD.

Six potatoes, one half of a small turnip, one half of a carrot, one small beet. Cut potatoes into small slices, the beet a little finer, and the turnip and carrot *very fine;* chop (with a *sharp* knife) a spoonful of green parsley. Mix all thoroughly, sprinkle with a scant teaspoonful of salt, unless the vegetables were salted in cooking, and then add the whole French dressing or half a cup of the boiled dressing. Keep very cool until it is served.

with a coarse grater, using a good deal of pressure. Two strokes will give about two drops of juice, which will be about enough for the above rule.

POTATO SALAD.

Ten potatoes cut fine, the French dressing, with four or five drops of onion juice in it, one table-spoonful of chopped parsley.

LETTUCE SALAD.

Two small or one large heads of lettuce; break all the leaves off carefully and wash each one separately and then throw them in a pan of ice water, where they should stand at least an hour; then put them in a wire basket or a coarse towel and *shake* out all the water. Either cut with a very sharp knife or tear into large pieces. Mix the French dressing with this and serve immediately. Beets, cucumbers, tomatoes, cauliflower, asparagus, etc., can be each served as a salad with the French or boiled dressing. Cold potatoes and cold beef, mutton or lamb, cut up fine and finished with either dressing, make a nice salad.

ADDITIONAL SALADS.

RICH SALAD DRESSING.

One table-spoonful of mustard, one table-spoonful of sugar, one tenth of a teaspoonful of cayenne pepper, one teaspoonful of salt, yolks of three uncooked eggs, juice of half a lemon, one quarter of a cup of vinegar, one pint of oil, one cup of whipped cream.

Beat yolks of eggs and the dry ingredients (until they are very light and thick) either with a silver or wooden spoon, or, better still, with a second sized Dover beater; then add a few drops of oil at a time until it becomes very *thick* and rather hard : after it has come to that stage the oil can be added more rapidly. When it gets so thick that the beater turns hard, add a little vinegar. When the last of the oil and vinegar is added it should be *very thick*. Now add the lemon juice and the whipped cream, and set away on the ice for a few hours, unless you are ready to use it. The bowl in which the dressing is made should set in a pan of ice water all the time it is being beaten. The cream may be omitted.

LOBSTER SALAD.

Lobster salad is made by cutting the lobster rather fine with a sharp knife ; then, for every quart of lobster, mixing two table-spoonfuls of vinegar, a teaspoonful of salt, one half of pepper, and seasoning the lobster with it. Now set away on the ice for an hour or two. Prepare the lettuce the same as for lettuce salad ; add to the lobster, at the time of serving, in the proportion of half as much lettuce as lobster ; season to taste with dressing. About half a pint of dressing to three pints of salad.

CHICKEN SALAD.

Made the same as lobster, using chicken instead of lobster, and celery instead of lettuce.

BAKED BEANS.

Examine and wash one quart of dry beans (the pea bean is the best for baking), and put them in a pan with six quarts of cold water; let them soak over night. In the morning wash them in another water, and place them on the fire with six quarts of cold water and a pound of mixed salt pork. If they are the present year's beans they will cook enough in half an hour, if older one hour. Drain, and put half of them in the bean-pot; then put in the pork which you have scored, and now the remainder of the beans, one table-spoonful of salt, and one of molasses; cover with boiling water. Bake very slowly for ten hours, adding boiling water whenever the beans begin to grow dry.

STEWED BEANS.

Wash and soak over night one quart of beans (scarlet runners are the best). In the morning set them on the fire with half a pound of mixed salt pork. They will cook in four hours, but are better cooked five; if the pork does not flavor it enough season with a little salt.

EIGHTH LESSON.

POULTRY.

TO CLEAN POULTRY.

FIRST singe over blazing paper or alcohol; then cut off the feet and tips of the wings, and the neck as far as it looks dark; then, with the blade of a knife take out all the pin-feathers; turn the skin of the neck back, and with the forefinger and thumb draw out the crop and windpipe; cut a slit in the lower part of the fowl, and draw out the intestines, being careful not to break the gall-bag, as it will spoil the flavor of the meat. It will be found near the upper part of the breast-bone and attached to the liver. Wash thoroughly in several waters, and drain. If the poultry is at all strong, let it stand in water several hours, with either charcoal or saleratus. Split the gizzard, and take out the inside and inner lining; wash, and put on to boil in two quarts of cold water (this for the gravy).

ROAST TURKEY.

Prepare as directed; make a dressing with six pounded crackers, one teaspoonful of pepper, one table-spoonful of salt, one teaspoonful of sage, one of summer savory, one of parsley, two eggs, butter the size of an egg, and cold water to moisten; stuff the turkey with this; stuff the breast first, and the remainder put in the body. Now cross and tie the legs down tight; run a skewer through the wings, fastening them to the body; fasten the neck under the body with a skewer, and tie all with twine. Rub the turkey with salt, and spit it; baste often with the drippings and flour, and occasionally with butter. About fifteen minutes before dishing baste with butter, and dredge on a little flour; this will give it a frothy appearance. For eight pounds, allow one hour and three quarters, if roasted in the tin-kitchen; if in the oven, one hour and a half, and fifteen minutes for every pound more. Serve with giblet gravy and cranberry sauce.

To make the gravy: Boil the heart, gizzard, liver, and neck in two quarts of water two hours; then take them up and chop the gizzard and heart, braid the liver, and put them back again; thicken with one table-spoonful of flour wet with cold water; season with salt and pepper. Let this simmer one hour longer, and when you dish the turkey turn the drippings into this gravy; boil up once, and send to the table. Make all the gravy for poultry in this manner, omitting the chopped gizzards in chicken gravy.

ROAST CHICKEN.

Prepare, stuff, and truss the same as turkey. A pair of chickens, weighing each two and a half pounds, will require an hour and a quarter to roast if in the tin-kitchen; one hour, if in the oven.

ROAST GOOSE.

Prepare as directed for poultry, and stuff the body with a dressing made in the following manner: Pare and boil ten potatoes; mash them and mix with one fourth of an onion chopped fine one table-spoonful of sage, one of salt, one teaspoonful of pepper, a small piece of butter. Truss, and roast (if it weighs ten pounds) one hour and three quarters if in the tin-kitchen, but if in the oven one hour and a half. Make the gravy as for turkey, and serve with apple sauce.

Skim off all the fat before putting the drippings in the gravy.

ROAST DUCK.

Prepare the dressing as for goose, and roast before a hot fire forty minutes, or if in the oven have it very hot and roast thirty minutes. Serve with either apple-sauce or currant jelly. Make gravy the same as for turkey.

This time cooks the goose and ducks rare.

ROAST PARTRIDGES.

Clean and truss; then lard and roast thirty minutes. Serve with currant jelly. To make the gravy: Put one table-spoonful of butter into a basin, and when it boils up stir in one table-spoonful of dry flour; stir until a dark brown; then pour on half a pint of boiling water. Season with salt, pepper, the partridge drippings, and a table-spoonful of currant jelly. Or, serve with bread sauce, the rule for which you will find under sauces.

To lard a bird: Cut fat salt pork into thin, narrow

slices, and put one end of the slice through the eye of a larding needle. (You can obtain one at any kitchen furnishing store.) Now run the needle under the skin of the bird, and draw the pork half way through, having the pieces about an inch apart.

ROAST GROUSE.

If you stuff them, make the dressing the same as for turkey; but they are not often stuffed. Roast thirty minutes, and serve with currant jelly. The gravy made the same as before directed.

ROAST PIGEONS.

Lard and roast the same as partridges. Make the gravy the same, with the addition of one fifth of a teaspoonful of clove and half a wineglassful of claret. The pigeons must be young, or they will not be nice roasted.

SMALL BIRDS.

Woodcock, quail, snipe, and plover may be cooked in the same manner as partridges, allowing fifteen minutes to roast. Serve on toast.

NINTH LESSON.

SAUCES.

DRAWN BUTTER.

BEAT one cup of butter and two table-spoonfuls of flour to a cream, and pour over this one pint of boiling water. Set on the fire and let it come to a boil, but do *not boil*. Serve immediately.

EGG SAUCE.

Chop up two hard-boiled eggs, and stir into drawn butter.

OYSTER SAUCE.

Set a basin on the fire with half a pint of oysters and one pint of boiling water; let them boil three minutes, and then stir in half a cup of butter beaten to a cream, with two table-spoonfuls of flour; let this come to a boil, and serve.

CELERY SAUCE.

Chop fine two heads of celery, and boil one hour; at the end of that time have about a pint and a half of water with it, and stir in two table-spoonfuls of flour wet with cold water. Boil this ten minutes, and then stir in two table-spoonfuls of butter. Season with pepper and salt, and serve.

CAPER SAUCE.

Into a pint of drawn butter stir three table-spoonfuls of capers.

MINT SAUCE.

Chop fine half a cupful of mint, and add to it a cup of vinegar and a table-spoonful of sugar.

CREAM SAUCE.

One cup of milk, one teaspoonful of flour, one table-spoonful of butter, salt, pepper.

Put one table spoonful of butter into a small frypan, and when it gets hot, but *not brown*, add the flour; stir until perfectly smooth; then add *gradually* the cold milk; let it boil up once, season to taste with salt and pepper, and serve. This is nice to cut cold potatoes into and let them just heat through; they are then called *creamed potatoes;* also for a sauce for vegetables, for omelets, for fish, for sweet-breads, or, indeed, for anything that requires a white sauce. If you have plenty of cream use that and omit the butter.

BREAD SAUCE, FOR GAME.

Two cups of milk, one cup dried bread crumbs, one quarter of an onion, two table-spoonfuls of butter, salt, pepper.

Dry the bread in a warm oven, and then roll into rather coarse crumbs; now sift them, and the fine crumbs which come through the sieve, and which make about one third of a cupful; put on to boil with the milk and onion; boil ten or fifteen minutes, then add one table-spoonful of butter, and seasoning, skim out the onion. Fry the coarse crumbs a light crisp brown in one table-spoonful of butter, which must be *very hot* before the crumbs are added. Stir over a hot fire for two minutes, being careful not to burn. Cover the breast of the roast birds with these, and serve the sauce poured around the birds or in a gravy dish.

TOMATO SAUCE.

One quart of canned tomatoes, two table-spoonfuls of butter, two of flour, eight whole cloves, one small slice of onion.

Cook tomatoes ten minutes with onion and cloves. Heat the butter in a small frypan and add the flour; stir over the fire until smooth and brown; then stir into the tomatoes, season to taste with salt and pepper, *rub* through a strainer which is fine enough to keep back all the seeds. This sauce is nice for fish, meat, and macaroni.

HOLLANDAISE SAUCE.

One half teacupful of butter, juice of half a lemon, yolks of two eggs, a speck of Cayenne pepper, one half cup of boiling water, one half teaspoonful of salt.

Beat butter to a cream, then add yolks of eggs one by one, then lemon juice, pepper, and salt. Now place the bowl in which is the mixture in a saucepan of boiling water, beat with an egg beater until it begins to thicken, which will be in about one minute; then add boiling water, beating all the time; as soon as it is like a soft custard it is done. It will take about five minutes over the fire if the bowl is thin and the water boils all the time. For fish and meats, to be poured around the article on the dish.

MILK SAUCE FOR FISH.

One and a half pints of milk, two table-spoonfuls of flour, one half of butter, one half of a small onion, two sprigs of parsley, one heaping teaspoonful of salt, a speck of pepper.

Put a pint of milk on to boil, with the onion and parsley, mix the flour to a smooth paste with part of the half pint of milk; then add the rest to make it very thin, and when the milk boils stir this into it; let it boil ten minutes longer, then add butter and salt, and strain.

APPLE SAUCE.

Pare, quarter, and core nice tart apples. Make a syrup of two quarts of water and one cup of sugar; simmer the apples in this until tender, but do not break them; then lay in an earthen dish; do this until they are all cooked (do not put many in the syrup at a time), and then let the syrup get cool, and turn on the apples.

BAKED PEARS.

Put the pears in a deep earthen dish or a baking pan, and to a dozen good-sized pears allow half a cup of sugar and a pint and a half of water. Bake in a moderate oven two hours and a half, or three. They will not keep many days cooked in this manner, but they are nice. Sweet apples are cooked in the same manner.

STEWED PRUNES.

Wash the prunes in warm water and rub them well between the hands. Put them in a kettle that you can cover tight, with two quarts of water to one of prunes. Stew them gently two hours. These will not keep more than two days in warm weather, but cooked in this way they do not require any sugar, and are very nice.

CODDLED APPLES.

Pare and core with an apple corer, cook the same as for apple sauce; but allow one pint of sugar to one quart of water.

CRANBERRY SAUCE.

Pick and wash the cranberries, and put in the preserving kettle with half a pint of water to one quart of berries; now put the sugar on top of the berries, allowing a pint of sugar to a quart of berries. Set on the fire and stew about half an hour. Stir often to prevent burning. They will not need straining, and will preserve their rich color cooked in this way. Never cook cranberries before putting in the sugar. Less sugar may be used if you do not wish them very rich.

TENTH LESSON.

OMELETS.

BEAT lightly two eggs, and stir in one table-spoonful of milk and a pinch of salt. Heat the omelet pan hot, and then put in half a table-spoonful of butter, and when melted turn in the beaten eggs; set on the fire, shake the pan, cook until a light brown; then fold the omelet and serve on a hot dish. Ham, mushroom, lobster, chicken, and all kinds of omelets are made by chopping up the meat, and laying it between the folds before dishing.

QUAKER OMELET.

Three eggs, one and a half table-spoonfuls of corn starch, half a cup of milk, half a teaspoonful of salt, one table-spoonful of butter.

Put a good sized omelet or frypan, with a tin cover, on to heat. Beat the yolks of the eggs, the salt, and the corn starch together; then beat the whites to a stiff froth, add to the yolks, then add the milk; butter the hot pan with the table-spoonful of butter, pour the mixture in, and cover with the hot cover; keep where it will not burn, but will brown, for about seven minutes, fold and serve on a hot dish. This omelet is improved by having the cream sauce poured around it.

OYSTER STEW.

Drain all the liquor from the oysters; put it into a porcelain kettle, and let it come to a boil; then skim off all the scum. Now turn in the milk, which you have let come to a boil in hot water. (Allow one quart of milk to one pint of oysters.) Stir in also one table-spoonful of butter or more, salt and pepper to taste. Now put in the oysters, let them boil up once, and serve with a dish of oyster crackers.

OYSTER SOUP.

Wash one quart of oysters, if they are solid, in one quart of cold water; if not, one pint of water; drain the water through a colander into the soup-kettle; set the kettle on the fire, and when the liquor comes to a boil skim it; then add one quart of rich new milk; just before it comes to a boil, turn in the oysters, and thicken with two table-spoonfuls of corn starch wet with milk; then stir in half a cup of butter, and season with pepper and salt. Let this boil up once, and serve immediately. Be very careful that they do not burn. A safe way is to boil the milk in a basin, which is set into another of water, and then turn it on the oysters just before removing it from the fire.

SCALLOPED OYSTERS.

Put a layer of oysters in an oval dish, and dredge in a little salt and pepper, and lay on a few small pieces of butter; then a layer of rolled crackers, and another of oysters; dredge the oysters as before, and cover with cracker; over the cracker lay on small pieces of butter. Bake twenty minutes in a quick oven. Allow four crackers, two table-spoonfuls of butter, and one teaspoonful of pepper to one quart of oysters. Fill the dish to within an inch of the top.

FRIED OYSTERS.

Drain the oysters on a sieve; roll them in cracker crumbs, and fry in boiling lard a light brown. Serve on brown-bread toast. When you desire them fried in batter, make one as for apple fritters, and fry in boiling lard. Have the dishes very hot.

BROILED OYSTERS.

Prepare in crumbs as for frying, and broil a light brown. Examine oysters carefully to see that there are not pieces of shell among them. Some oysters need more salt than others.

MACARONI, BOILED.

Break up and wash a pint bowl full of macaroni, and put in a shallow basin, and cover with cold water. Set this basin into another of warm water, and place on the fire; after fifteen minutes, add a pint of milk and a teaspoonful of salt; let it cook ten minutes longer, then add a table-spoonful of butter, and cook five minutes more, and dish. Be careful not to break the macaroni in dishing. The boiled macaroni which remains from one dinner can be used for the next, by preparing it in the following manner: Butter a shallow dish, and turn the macaroni into it; than grate over it old cheese, and brown.

MILK TOAST.

Put one quart of milk on to boil. Mix two table-spoonfuls of flour with half a cup of cold milk, stir this into the boiling milk and let it boil ten minutes, then add one table-spoonful of butter, and one large teaspoonful of salt. Now dip the bread in, and serve. The bread must be toasted as carefully for this as for dry toast. . The bread must be stale to make good toast.

BAKED CUSTARD.

One quart milk, four table-spoonfuls of sugar, four eggs, one teaspoonful of salt, a little nutmeg.

Beat sugar, salt, and eggs together with a spoon, then add the milk. Fill the custard cups, grate on a little nutmeg, and place the cups in a deep baking pan, then nearly fill the pan with warm water. Bake in a moderate oven till firm in the centre. It will take from twenty to forty minutes to bake them, all depending upon the heat of the oven. The slower they bake the richer and smoother they will be. Try them by running a knife through the centre; if they are firm they are done.

STEAMED CUSTARDS.

Steamed custards are made the same as baked, only that they are steamed from twelve to fifteen min utes over a kettle of boiling water.

ELEVENTH LESSON.

SICK-ROOM COOKERY.

ONE of the things which every woman ought to know, no matter what her station in life, is how to cook for the sick, and also how to care for them and their rooms. Some of the first necessities of the sick are quiet, fresh air, and cleanliness; the next is proper food, properly cooked, and given at the right time. Many persons wonder why they do not get well, and blame the physician for their long illness, when all the trouble is that they do not have fresh air enough, they are not bathed often enough, their own and the bed linen are not changed often enough. They see too many people, and their food is not of the right kind nor cooked properly. I am sure that many kind people would be terribly shocked if they were told that they had killed their friends, and yet it is being done every day simply by the neglect of the simplest remedies. Then remember and keep plenty of fresh air in the sick-room, keep it clean and quiet, wash the patient every day; if there is fever use a little soda in the water, only wash a small part of the body at a time, and keep the rest covered. A sponge to wash with and a soft towel to wipe with, keep both sponge and towels perfectly clean and fresh. Do *not*

SICK-ROOM COOKERY

whisper or walk on tiptoes in a sick-room. If you have anything to say that you do not wish the patient to hear *leave the room*. There is nothing that is more trying to a sick person than to have a conversation which he cannot understand going on in the room. If you employ a physician *follow his directions exactly;* if you cannot do that, it is just as well not to have one; remember that he has made the study and practice of medicine a life-work, and there is every reason for believing that he knows more about the case than you do. When the physician asks for a report of the symptoms of the patient, be sure that you give them, as far as you can remember, truthfully. These remarks may seem out of place in a lesson on cookery, but as sick-room cookery nearly always devolves upon the person who takes care of the sick, it seems that this is as good as any place.

Do not cook much of anything. A well person tires of one dish soon, and a sick person is much more liable to do so. Do not feel vexed if after much care and labor you have prepared an article and the patient will not touch it. Always keep in mind that a sick person is never reasonable, and do as you would be done by. Do not keep a patient waiting for his food.

BEEF TEA.

Cut half a pound of lean beef into very small pieces; do not have a grain of fat on it, and put into a bottle that has a large opening (an olive or horseradish bottle will be nice); put in half a cup of cold water, and cork tight; set this in a basin of cold water, and place on the fire where it will come to a boiling point, but not boil; keep it at this temperature for two hours, then strain, and season with salt.

ANOTHER BEEF TEA.

Cut half a pound of lean beef (the round is the best) into dice. Put into a saucepan, with a teaspoonful of salt, one of flour, and one fourth of pepper. Pour on this a large pint of cold water. Let it stand an hour or two, then put on the fire; bring slowly to a boil, and boil slowly for an hour. If it has boiled away too much, add a little hot water; but this rather hurts it. Skim off carefully every particle of fat. This tea is more palatable than the other, and can be taken by those not extremely sick.

SACK POSSET.

Pound one Boston cracker, or one soda biscuit. Put it in a pint of cold milk; set it on the fire, and simmer fifteen minutes. Beat together one egg, one wineglass of wine, a little sugar, salt, and nutmeg. Turn this into the simmering milk, stirring constantly; boil up once, and take from the fire immediately.

CHICKEN BROTH.

Put the bones and about one pound of the lean meat of chicken into a saucepan with three pints of water. When it comes to a boil, skim well. Simmer three hours, and strain and salt. If the patient can bear it, a little rice or tapioca boiled with it is an improvement.

SICK-ROOM COOKERY.

OATMEAL GRUEL.

Into one quart of boiling water sprinkle two table-spoonfuls of oatmeal; let this boil forty minutes; season with salt, strain, and serve. If sugar, milk, or cream is wished, it may be added.

INDIAN MEAL GRUEL.

One quart of boiling water; stir into this one tablespoonful of flour and two of Indian meal, mixed with a little cold water. Boil thirty minutes. Season with salt, and strain. Use sugar and cream if you choose. If flour is not liked use another table-spoonful of meal instead.

PLUM PORRIDGE.

Into one quart of boiling milk stir two table-spoonfuls of flour mixed with cold milk; put in a handful of raisins and a little grated nutmeg. Boil twenty minutes. Season with salt, and strain.

CORN TEA.

Brown, and pound in a mortar, one cup of sweet dry corn; pour on this two cups of boiling water, and steep fifteen minutes. This is very light and nutritious, and can be taken when the patient is very weak.

WINE WHEY.

Let one cup of new milk come to boil, and then stir in half a wineglass of sherry wine. Boil a moment and strain.

VINEGAR WHEY.

Boil one cup of milk, and stir in one table-spoonful of vinegar; if this does not make it whey, stir in a little more; when it curdles, strain.

SOUR MILK WHEY.

To one cup of boiling sweet milk, add one cup of sour milk, and strain.

TWELFTH LESSON.

SICK-ROOM COOKERY. — *Continued.*

BEEFSTEAK.

HAVE a very small piece of sirloin steak cut rather thick. When everything is ready on the tray, put the steak over a clear coal fire to broil; cook eight minutes; season with salt; dish on a warm plate, and serve *immediately*.

MUTTON OR LAMB CHOP.

Mutton or lamb chops are cooked and served the same way as beefsteak, only first trimming off all the fat.

If the patient cannot eat rare meat, have the steak and chops cut rather thin.

CREAM TOAST.

Let half a cup of cream come to a boil, and season with salt. Have two slices of bread toasted a nice brown; dip them in the cream, and dish; pour the remaining cream over them. Serve immediately.

RICE COFFEE.

Brown rice as you would the coffee bean, and then either grind or mash in the mortar; take half a cup of the ground rice, and pour about a quart of boiling water over it and let it stand about ten or fifteen minutes; then strain and sweeten with loaf sugar and season with boiled milk. Drink of this freely. This is particularly nice for children.

FLOUR GRUEL.

Let one quart of fresh milk come to a boil, and then stir in one table-spoonful of flour which has been mixed with milk enough to make a smooth paste; boil this mixture thirty minutes, being careful not to let it burn. Season with salt and strain. The patient should be kept warm and quiet.

CUSTARD.

Whites of three eggs, one quarter teaspoonful of salt, two table-spoonfuls of sugar, a light grating of nutmeg, one pint of rich new milk.

Beat sugar, whites of eggs, salt, and nutmeg together; then add a little milk; beat a few minutes longer; add the remainder of the milk; turn into custard cups, and bake in a slow oven in a pan of warm water until they are firm in the centre.

EGGNOG.

One egg, one table-spoonful of sugar, one of water, one of milk, one of wine.

Beat the white of the egg to a stiff froth; then beat in the sugar; next the yolk; then milk and wine.

A GOOD DRINK FOR THE LUNGS.

Wash clean a few pieces of Irish moss ; put it in a pitcher, and pour over it two cups of boiling water. Set where it will keep at the boiling point, but not boil, for two hours. Strain, and squeeze into it the juice of one lemon. Sweeten to taste. If the patient cannot take lemon, flavor with wine, vanilla, or nutmeg.

ANOTHER DRINK.

Beat lightly one egg and one table-spoonful of sugar. Stir into this one cup of new milk, half a wineglass of wine, and a little nutmeg. This is nice without the wine.

ANOTHER DRINK.

Upon one teaspoonful of slippery-elm pour one cup of boiling water, strain, and season as Irish moss.

LEMONADE.

The juice of one lemon and one table-spoonful of sugar. Pour on this one cup of boiling water, and set away to cool.

CURE FOR HOARSENESS.

Bake a lemon or sour orange for twenty minutes in a moderate oven, then open it at one end and dig out the inside, which sweeten with sugar or molasses, and eat. This will cure hoarseness and remove pressure from the lungs.

BURNS.

Rub a little oil or butter on the burned part, and cover with soda. This is for slight burns, which many are always getting in the kitchen. If the air is kept from burns and cuts they will heal rapidly; for this reason burns are often covered with glue.

UNFAILING CURE FOR CONSTIPATION.

Three teacupfuls of coarse, clean wheat-bran, three of sifted flour, one heaping teaspoonful of cream of tartar, one half of soda, one of salt, seven of sweet butter. Mix with cold milk and roll into thin biscuit, and bake thoroughly in a moderately hot oven. They should be from one fourth to one third of an inch thick, and be cut with a small biscuit cutter.

Great care must be taken that they do not burn, and at the same time that they get *thoroughly baked*. They will keep a long time if kept in a tight tin box; they should be eaten at each meal. — *From Mr. Leonard Scott, after twenty years' experience.*

CURE NO. 2.

A little while before retiring, mix a table-spoonful of flaxseed in cold water enough to make it pour readily, and on going to bed drink this. It is not nauseating at all, and will act on the bowels without deranging them as drugs always do.

Drinking a glass of cold water at night and in the morning helps many persons. Eating fruit is also good.

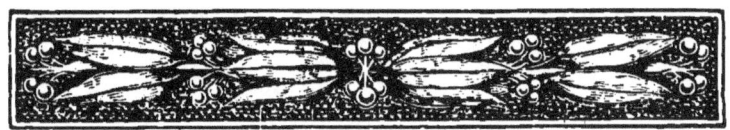

MISCELLANEOUS ARTICLES.

REMARKS ON DIGESTION.

In the stomach is produced a liquid secretion called the gastric juice. This does not act upon starch or fat of any kind. The only thing it dissolves is the albuminous matter. Now, when this albuminous matter is not saturated with fat, the gastric juice acts upon it readily; but as in the case of pastry, doughnuts, fried meats, etc., where the whole mass is saturated with a fatty substance, it takes a long time before the gastric juice can get at the albuminous matter to act upon it: hence the distress by the overworking of the stomach; and if this kind of food is partaken of frequently the stomach force will be weakened and refuse to do its work. This will disarrange every other member of the digestive organs, and, in a short time, you have a first-class dyspeptic. All food, therefore, should be as light, porous, and free from fat as possible.

When fat is used, it should be in such a manner that it will separate readily from the other substances on entering the stomach. Alcohol retards digestion, and renders it incomplete, by coagulating the gastric juice. Food, when taken into the stomach either *very* hot or *very* cold, does not digest readily. Food taken when the body or mind is very tired does not digest readily. Digestion goes on very slowly during sleep, but it is more complete, and repairs the waste of the body more thoroughly than the rapid digestion of the waking hours. Children digest food more rapidly than adults, and should, therefore, be given a light lunch when more than four hours intervene between the regular meals.

It is a great mistake to think that light breakfasts are better than substantial ones. The breakfast supplies the fuel for the great waste which goes on during the busiest part of the day, and therefore should be of a simple, nutritious character, and an abundant supply of it. Another mistake made by many persons is the taking of a number of hours of exercise before breakfast.

The stomach, while empty, is in a condition to receive disease. In a high, dry atmosphere, there is less danger from this habit; but in a country which is at all malarious it is one of the most dangerous things which can be done.

Regularity as to the time of eating is also one of the necessary things to be observed, that the digestion may be perfect. Pastry should be used very sparingly, puddings, fruits, and light desserts taking the place of pies.

The preparation of food should be made more a matter of conscience, with the housekeeper and cook, than it is at present. In planning the preparation of a dish the questions should not be, Is it convenient? and Will it please? but, Will it be healthful, mentally, morally, and physically? for the food we eat affects the three natures.

Then food, to do its highest and best work, must be of the best quality, prepared carefully (but always to retain its simplest form), partaken of regularly in a cheerful room and in cheerful company.

REMARKS.

Always measure flour after it has been sifted, unless told to measure before. Always sift Indian and rye meal, and never sift Graham or oatmeal. Always set milk into boiling water to boil, as it boils quicker in this way, and there will be no danger of burning. Save all the fat from soups, boiled and roast meats. The fat from beef, pork, and poultry keep for shortening or frying; and from ham, mutton, and soups, in which vegetables were boiled, for the soap grease. To clarify drippings, boil them a few minutes, and then cut in a raw potato and let it cook for five minutes, then drop in a pinch of saleratus, and strain. If all the drippings are taken care of it will be a great saving in a family. In many of the rules given here it has been very difficult to say just how much spice to use, as there is such a difference in tastes, so that each one must use her own judgment; but be careful that no one spice predominates. Always use twice as much cinnamon and nutmeg as you do clove. In making frosting, pudding sauce, and all kinds of delicate cake, use the powdered sugar, if possible. For rich cake, the coffee-crushed, powdered and sifted, is the best. For dark cake, the brown sugar will be found the nicest. It makes it richer. Save all the pieces of bread for dressing, puddings, and griddle-cakes. Tin is not very good to mix cake in, and earthen dishes are always being broken. The stone china wash bowls are very good for this purpose. You can often find odd ones at the crockery stores, and they will last a lifetime for this purpose. In baking and frying cook everything *brown*. Bread and pastry are more healthful overdone than underdone.

One even quart of sifted flour is one pound; one pint of granulated sugar is one pound; two good-sized cups of butter are one pound. Do not buy large quantities of Indian and rye meal at a time, as they sour quickly. Keep all kinds of meal, flour, and meats in a cool, dry place. Keep tea, coffee, and extracts from the air. Never set anything into the ice-chest while warm, as it will heat the chest and absorb an unpleasant flavor from the chest. This is true of the cellar also. Keep a note-book for tried receipts, and for any changes which you wish to make in the receipts which you are constantly using. By thought and observation one can learn something new in regard to cooking every day, and at the time it will seem so important that you cannot forget it; but you will if you do not have it written.

ARTICLES FOR COOKING ROOM.

Large stove or range, — a stove is better than a range; two large tables, one dish pan, two rather small bread pans, four yellow bowls, from six quarts down; four white smooth-bottom bowls, two muffin pans, each containing twelve cups; four tin baking pans, two Russia iron baking pans, four large cooking spoons, six teaspoons, two table-spoons, one carving-knife, one butcher's knife, one large carving-fork, two vegetable knives, two case knives, one second size Dover beater, one common wire beater, one bread board, one rolling-pin, six cups, holding half a pint each; two quart measures, one biscuit cutter, four deep tin plates, three wire toasters, one for fish, one for meat, and one for bread; one bean-pot, one pudding-dish, three frypans, Nos. 1, 3, and 6; three porcelain-lined stewpans, from two quarts to four; two two-quart tin basins, a hand-basin, three tin saucepans, one one pint, one three pints, one three quarts; meat rack, four bread-pans, one double kettle, one wire dishcloth, one linen dishcloth, four long towels for lifting pans, twelve dish towels, four rollers, one colander, one vegetable masher, one sieve, one strainer, one coffee-pot, one filter, one tea-pot, one chocolate pot, one deep Scotch kettle for frying, meat and bread boards, pail, broom, brush, dust-pan, duster, floor-cloth, sink-cloth, soap-dish, blacking brush, brown bread tin, steamer, dishes enough to set a table in the simplest manner, chopping-tray and knife.

If more than the simplest things are taught, of course a greater variety of utensils will be required.

ADDITIONAL RECEIPTS.

SOUPS AND STEWS.

SMALL, tough pieces of meat can be served in no more nutritious and satisfactory forms than as soups and stews. These dishes, if carefully prepared, are savory, economical, and healthful. One thing must always be heeded in order to insure success : cook the dishes *slowly*. In this one word lies the secret of much of the success it is possible to secure. Onions, when cooked a long time, or fried in fat before being put into a soup or stew, acquire an unequaled rich and mellow flavoring quality. But the cooking should be so thorough that their presence in the dish cannot be detected. Pork is frequently named in this book for use in soups, stews, and fricassees, but if any other kind of fat be preferred or be more convenient, it can be substituted.

PEA SOUP.

One quart of dried peas, seven quarts of water, two large onions, one pound of lean salt pork, one stalk of celery, three whole cloves, salt, pepper. Pick over the peas, and wash thoroughly ; then put them in three quarts of cold water, and let them soak all night. In the morning pour off all the water, and put the peas in the soup-kettle with seven quarts of cold water, the pork, and other ingredients. Boil gently seven hours. Take out the pork, and rub the soup through a sieve. Serve with toasted bread and the boiled pork. If pork be not liked, a small piece of the neck of beef may be used, — about two pounds. The soup must be stirred frequently to prevent burning.

BEAN SOUP.

One pint of dried beans, four quarts of water, one onion, half a pound of salt pork, salt, pepper. Wash the beans, and soak all night in three quarts of cold water. In the morning pour off all the water and wash the beans in two waters. This prevents the rank flavor in the soup. Now put the pork and beans on to boil in four quarts of cold water. Boil gently six hours. Season with salt and pepper, and rub through a strainer. Return to the fire, and boil up once. Put one table-spoonful of butter or drippings in a saucepan, and when hot add one table-spoonful of flour. Cook this until it is a light brown ; then stir into the soup, and boil five minutes longer. Serve with toasted bread and the pork.

ONION SOUP.

Six large onions, one quart of milk, one quart of water, six table-spoonfuls of cracker crumbs, four table-spoonfuls of flour, a quarter of a pound of fat salt pork, salt, pepper. Cut the pork into thin slices, and fry slowly in the soup-kettle. When it is thoroughly fried, add the onions, which have been cut into *thin* slices, and fry slowly until these are a golden brown. They should cook about half an hour before they take this color. When they become brown, stir the dry flour in with them, and cook ten minutes longer, being careful not to let the onions turn dark brown. Now add one quart of boiling water, and simmer gently two hours (one hour will do, if more time cannot be given). Add the salt, pepper, and milk, and let the soup boil up once. Strain, and add the cracker crumbs. Boil three minutes, and serve.

SHIN OF BEEF SOUP.

Six pounds of the shin of beef, three onions, one turnip, one carrot, half a cupful of rice, six potatoes, a few leaves of celery, one quart of finely-shred cabbage, salt, pepper, seven quarts of cold water. Having had the shin-bone cracked, wash it, and place it in the soup-kettle over a slow fire for about twenty minutes. Stir often. Now add the onions, sliced thin, and cook ten minutes longer, stirring frequently. Add the cold water, and when it comes to the boiling point, skim. Simmer two hours, and then add the carrot, turnip, and cabbage, all cut fine. Simmer two hours longer, and add the rice, potatoes, salt, and pepper. Cook one hour longer, and serve. Barley may be used instead of rice, but in that case it should be added with the cold water, as it requires a great deal of cooking.

VEGETABLE SOUP.

Two quarts of finely-shred cabbage, three large onions, one large turnip, one carrot, two stalks of celery four quarts of water, four table-spoonfuls of drippings, four table-spoonfuls of flour, salt, pepper, eight large potatoes. Have the vegetables pared, washed, and cut fine. Let them stand in cold water. Put the drippings in the soup-pot, and when hot add the onions. Cook slowly ten minutes; then add the dry flour. Stir well, and cook ten minutes longer. Now add the cold water and all the vegetables except the potatoes. Simmer two hours. Add the potatoes and salt and pepper, and cook an hour longer. Five minutes before serving put six slices of stale bread in the soup. Any common kind of vegetable that is in the market can be used for this soup. The more kinds, the better the flavor.

CLAM SOUP.

One quart of clams, one of milk, one pint of water, three table-spoonfuls of butter, three of flour, four of cracker crumbs, salt, pepper. Separate the black heads from the clams, and put them on to simmer for half an hour in the pint of water. Chop the soft part of the clams, and put aside. Rub the butter and flour together, and stir into the boiling clams; then add the milk, salt, and pepper. Let this mixture boil up, and then strain upon the chopped part óf the clams. Return to the fire, and boil three minutes. Add the cracker crumbs, and serve.

CLAM CHOWDER.

One quart of clams, one quart of pared and *thinly*-sliced potatoes, two onions, a quarter of a pound of salt pork, six soft crackers, one quart of water, one quart of milk, three table-spoonfuls of flour, salt, pepper. Separate the black heads from the soft part of the clams, and simmer them in the water for half an hour. Fry the pork slowly, and when brown and dry, add the onions, cut fine. Fry slowly until the onions are a pale straw color; then add the dry flour, and cook two minutes, stirring all the while. Stir into the water in which the heads are boiling. Put in the soup-kettle a layer of potatoes, then one of the soft clams, and dredge well with salt and pepper; add a layer of crackers, and begin again with the potatoes and clams, and when all the ingredients have been used, strain over them the water in which the heads simmered. Cover closely, and simmer gently twenty minutes; then add the milk, and boil up once. If you would like the pork and onions in the chowder, strain the water in which the heads were cooked upon the onion, pork, and flour, instead of proceeding as first directed. When the clams are bought in the shell, a peck will be required. Wash them free from sand, cover them with boiling water, and let them stand until the shells open a little; now take the clams from the shells, and proceed as directed, save that the water which was poured over them must be used. All water may be used instead of part milk, if it be preferred.

SALT FISH CHOWDER.

One pint of dried salt fish, free from skin and bone, half a pound of salt pork, two onions, one quart of pared and thinly-sliced potatoes, six soft crackers, three pints of water, one pint of milk, two table-spoonfuls of flour. Wash the fish, cover with cold water, and soak over night. Cut the pork into dice, and fry crisp and brown ; then add the onions, which have been cut fine. Fry slowly till a golden brown. Put in the soup-pot a layer of fish, which has been broken into flakes, and a layer of potatoes. Dredge with salt, pepper, and flour, and spread part of the onion and pork over these layers. Now add a layer of split crackers. Continue in this way until all the ingredients are used ; then add the three pints of cold water. Let the chowder come slowly to the boiling point, and keep it there, although not allowing it to boil, for one hour; then add the milk, and cook half an hour longer, keeping the kettle where it will not boil. All water may be used instead of part milk.

POTATO CHOWDER.

Two quarts of pared and sliced potatoes, five large onions, half a pound of salt pork, two quarts of water, two table-spoonfuls of flour, salt and pepper to taste. Cut the pork into thin strips, and fry slowly until a light brown ; then add the onions, which have been pared and sliced very thin. Cook *slowly* until a light brown. Put a layer of the sliced potatoes in the soup-kettle, then a thin layer of the pork and onion, and dredge well with salt, pepper, and flour. Add another layer of potato, and continue as before. When all the ingredients are used add the water. Let the chowder come slowly to the boiling point, and simmer forty minutes.

CHICKEN CHOWDER.

One fowl, weighing about four pounds, one eighth of a pound of salt pork, two large onions, one quart of pared and sliced potatoes, eight soft crackers, two small slices of carrot, three table-spoonfuls of flour, salt and pepper to taste, three quarts of hot water. Singe and wash the fowl, and cut it into small pieces. Cut the pork into thin slices, and fry slowly until a dark brown ; then add the carrot and onions, which have been cut into *thin* slices. Cook slowly for fifteen minutes. Put the fowl, onion, carrot, and pork, with one quart of hot water, in the soup-kettle, and simmer *slowly* two hours. Add the salt, pepper, potatoes, the remaining water, and the flour (mixed with a little cold water), and cook slowly forty minutes. Split the crackers, and dip into cold water or milk ; then lay them on top of the chowder, and cook ten minutes longer. If the fowl be very tough and old, it will take four hours' cooking before the remainder of the water and the other ingredients are added. Dumplings instead of crackers can be cooked with this chowder.

TOMATO CHOWDER.

Two quarts of fresh tomatoes, pared and sliced, or one quart of canned tomatoes, two onions, one quart of boiling water, quarter of a pound of salt pork, one fourth of a cupful of rice, one table-spoonful of flour. Slice the pork, and fry till a light brown ; then add the onion, and when this is of a light straw color add the dry flour. Cook and stir for three minutes. Add the water, rice, and tomatoes, and simmer one hour. Season with salt and pepper.

PARSNIP STEW WITH DUMPLINGS.

Half a pound of salt pork, ten good-sized potatoes, three large parsnips, three quarts of water, one tablespoonful of flour, mixed with half a cupful of cold water, salt and pepper to taste. Cut the pork into thin strips; scrape and slice the parsnips. Boil the pork and parsnips gently in the water for one hour; then add the thickening, salt, pepper, and the potatoes, which have been pared and sliced. Boil half an hour, when add the dumplings, cooking *ten* minutes.

BARLEY STEW.

About half a pound of cooked or uncooked meat, three large onions, one quart of pared and sliced potatoes, one third of a cupful of barley, salt and pepper to taste, two quarts of water, rather scant, and two table-spoonfuls of flour. Cut the meat into little bits; slice the onions very fine; wash the barley. Put these and the water in a large saucepan, and let them come slowly to the boiling point. Skim the stew as soon as it begins to boil, and set back where it will just bubble for three hours; then add the flour, which has been mixed with a little cold water, the potatoes and salt and pepper. Simmer one hour longer. The cheapest part of beef, mutton, or veal can be used for this dish, or, what is quite as well, bits of cold roasted or broiled meat. If one has plenty of meat, it will of course give a richer and more nutritious stew to use a quantity larger than that named, although half a pound will produce a palatable and nutritious dish. Pieces of stale bread, added the last ten minutes of cooking, are a desirable addition.

IRISH STEW.

Three pounds of the cheap parts of mutton, two onions, one small white turnip, one small carrot, one quart of pared and sliced potatoes, two table-spoonfuls of flour, two quarts of hot water, salt and pepper to taste. Cut the mutton into small pieces, and pare and cut into thin slices the onions, turnip, and carrot. Put these in the soup-kettle, and dredge in the flour, salt, and pepper. Add the water, and let all come to the boiling point. Skim the stew, and set back where it will bubble for two hours; then add the potatoes, and cook forty-five minutes longer.

MUTTON STEW.

Four pounds of the cheap part of mutton, one onion, one quart of boiling water, three table-spoonfuls of flour, salt and pepper to taste, two slices of carrot, two of turnip. Cut the mutton into small pieces. Put three table-spoonfuls of the fat of the meat, cut into little bits, in the soup-kettle, and fry slowly; then add the vegetables, cut fine, and cook ten minutes longer. Add the meat, and cook ten minutes, stirring constantly. Add the boiling water, and after letting the stew come to the boiling point, skim it; then add the flour, which has been mixed with cold water. Season with salt and pepper, and simmer slowly for three hours. Rice or potatoes should be served with this dish.

CORNED BEEF STEW.

Two pounds of cold corned beef, one quart of cold boiled potatoes, sliced, two onions, two table-spoon fuls of flour, one quart of cold water. Cut the beef into thin slices, and trim off some of the fat. Put the fat in a large saucepan, and when it has been frying about twelve minutes add the onions, cut into thin slices. Fry slowly for ten minutes, and after stirring in the flour fry two minutes more, stirring all the while. Add the water gradually, and cook three minutes. Season well with salt and pepper. Put in a layer of potatoes, then one of meat, and dredge with salt and pepper. Continue in this way until all the potatoes and meat are used. Cover the saucepan, and simmer very gently for half an hour. Serve on a platter, being careful not to break the meat or potatoes.

SAUSAGE STEW.

One pound of pork sausage, in either the cake or in cases, two quarts of pared and sliced potatoes, one large onion, salt, pepper, one table-spoonful of flour, one quart of water. Shred the onion very fine. Put a layer of the potato in the stew-pan, then a light layer of the onion and the sausage, which should be cut into thin slices; and if the meat be in cases, the skin should be removed. Dredge with salt, pepper, and flour. Continue in this way until all the materials are used, and add the boiling water. Cover the stew-pan, and simmer three quarters of an hour.

VEAL STEW.

Four pounds of veal, from any of the cheap parts, one onion, one quart of boiling water, two table-spoonfuls of flour, salt and pepper to taste, quarter of a pound of salt pork. Cut the pork into slices, and fry slowly in the stew-pan. When it is a light brown add the onion, which has been cut into thin slices, and cook ten minutes. Cut the veal into small pieces, and dredge with salt, pepper, and flour. Put these ingredients in the stew-pan and stir over the fire for six minutes; then add the water. Mix the remainder of the flour with a little cold water, and stir into the gravy. Set the stew-pan where the contents will just bubble for three hours. Taste to see if seasoned enough. One teaspoonful of curry powder is a great improvement. It should be added just before the stew is taken from the fire. Always serve boiled rice with this dish when the curry is used.

FISH STEW.

Four pounds of any kind of cheap fish, one onion, quarter of a pound of salt pork, one quart of water, two table-spoonfuls of flour, salt and pepper to taste. Remove the head, tail, and skin of the fish. Slip a sharp knife between the flesh and the bones. Put the head, tail, and bones in a stew-pan with one quart of cold water, letting them come to the boiling point, and simmer for twenty minutes. Cut the pork and onion into thin slices. Fry the pork slowly until a light brown; then add the onion, and cook until a light straw color. Add the dry flour, and cook three minutes, stirring all the while, and strain upon it the water in which the bones and head were boiled. Boil five minutes, and season with salt and pepper. Have the fish cut into handsome pieces, which lay in the saucepan with the gravy. Cover, and simmer *very slowly* thirty minutes.

VEGETABLE STEW.

One head of cabbage, weighing about four pounds, one quart of pared and sliced turnips, one quart of potato, pared and sliced, half a pint of carrot, one quart of parsnips, half a pound of salt pork, salt, and pepper, two quarts of water. Cut the pork into slices. Put the cabbage in the bottom of the stew-pan, next the pork, then the turnip, carrot, and parsnip. Dredge each layer with salt, pepper, and flour. Add the water, boiling. Cover the stew-pan, and simmer two hours; then add the potatoes, and simmer half an hour longer.

STEWED BEEF.

Four pounds of meat from the lower part of the round, or any of the other cheap parts, four whole cloves, three fourths of a quart of boiling water, three table-spoonfuls of flour, salt and pepper to taste. Put the beef in the stew-pan, and, covering it, let it cook slowly on top of the stove for half an hour, turning it occasionally. Add the water. Mix the flour with a little cold water, and stir into the gravy. Season with salt and pepper. Cover closely, and place where it will simmer gently for three hours.

BRAISED BEEFSTEAK.

Two pounds of the tough part of the round, one onion, a clove, one pint of boiling water, one teaspoonful of corn-starch. Dredge the meat well with salt, pepper, and flour. Cut the onion into thin slices, which put in a small saucepan or baking-pan; and upon them lay the meat, covering closely. Place in a rather cool oven and cook half an hour; then add the boiling water and the clove. Cover, and return to the oven. Cook *very slowly* for two hours and a half, basting with the gravy in the pan, and dredging with salt, pepper, and flour six times while cooking. Take up the meat. Mix the corn-starch with a little cold water, and stir into the gravy. Cook, on top of the stove, four minutes. Strain over the meat, and serve. Any kind of meat, from any part of the animal, can be prepared in this manner. The time given will answer for a piece weighing four pounds, if it be flat. A piece weighing six or eight pounds, if thick, will require five hours' cooking. The meat must in no case be cooked rapidly. All kinds of vegetables may be used in this dish. The onion, if not liked, may be omitted. When the meat is very dry, a few slices of salt pork can be put in the bottom of the pan.

VEAL POT PIE.

Five pounds of veal, half a pound of salt pork, two quarts of boiling water, four table-spoonfuls of flour, and salt and pepper. Cut the meat into small pieces, and dredge thickly with salt, pepper, and flour. Cut the pork into slices, and fry in the stew-pan until a light brown; then put in the veal, and stir around in the stew-pan until browned. Add the boiling water. Let it come to the boiling point, and set back where it can simmer slowly for two hours and a half. Mix the remainder of the flour with cold water, and stir into the gravy. Taste to see if seasoned enough. Make the dumpling mixture according to the rule on page 75, and, rolling down to the thickness of about one third of an inch, cut into squares. Stir the mixture which is in the stew-pan, and draw forward where it will boil. Lay the squares in the kettle, and, covering closely, boil twelve minutes. Take the cakes up first ; then pour the meat and gravy on a platter, and arrange the cakes on top.

FRICASSEE OF VEAL, WITH BISCUIT.

Two pounds of veal, quarter of a pound of salt pork, one pint and a half of cold water, three table-spoonfuls of flour, salt and pepper to taste. Cut the pork into thin slices, and fry to a deep brown, in a frying-pan. Cut the veal into thin slices, and dredge with salt and pepper. Fry in the pork fat until brown. Be careful not to burn the fat. As soon as the veal is brown take it up, and put the dry flour with the hot fat. Stir until brown ; then add the water, slowly, stirring all the while. When the gravy boils up let it cook five minutes. Add the fried veal, and cover. Cook slowly for twelve or fifteen minutes. Have biscuit made according to half the rule given subsequently in the appendix, and bake them in thin, small cakes. Lay the veal on a platter and pour the gravy over it. Place the biscuits on and around the fricassee, and serve.

FRICASSEE OF COLD MEAT, WITH BAKED DUMPLINGS.

Three pints of any kind of cold meat cut into small pieces, one pint of water, one large table-spoonful of flour, two table-spoonfuls of butter, and salt and pepper. Put the butter in a small sauce-pan or frying-pan, and when hot add the dry flour, and stir until brown. Gradually add the water. Season well with salt and pepper. Put the meat in a deep earthen dish, and season with salt and pepper. Pour the gravy over it, and place in the oven. Make biscuit according to half the rule, and cut them into small, thin cakes. Take the dish of meat from the oven and lay the cakes on top of it. Return to the oven and bake fifteen minutes. Serve in the same dish.

ROLLED FLANK OF BEEF.

Five pounds of the fresh flank of beef, salt, pepper, one cupful of cracker.crumbs, one teaspoonful of summer savory, one table-spoonful of butter. Wipe the beef with a damp cloth, and dredge well with salt and pepper. Spread on a board, and if one part be thicker than another cut some of the meat from the thick portion and lay on the thin. Make a dressing with the cracker, summer savory, butter, salt, pepper, and cold water enough to make the cracker quite moist. After spreading the meat with this, roll it up and tie it, and pin in a cloth. Place in a stew-pan, and just cover with boiling water. Let this come to the boiling point, and then set back where it will just bubble for five hours. Let the meat partially cool in the water in which it was boiled. When it is nearly cold, take it up, and remove the cloth, but not the strings. When cold, the piece will cut into tender round slices. The water in which it was boiled will do for the foundation of a vegetable, rice, or tomato soup, or, if thickened with flour, will make a nice gravy.

BEEF'S HEART.

One heart, one cupful of stale bread, one onion, one slice of carrot, one of turnip, one table-spoonful of butter, two slices of pork, one pint and a half of water, one large table-spoonful of flour, one eighth of a teaspoonful of summer savory, salt, pepper. Wash the heart. Soak the bread in one third of a cupful of cold water, and then mix with it the summer savory, butter, one fourth of a teaspoonful of salt, and a little pepper. After stuffing the heart with this, tie a strong piece of cotton cloth over the larger end of it. Put one slice of the pork and all the vegetables in a deep sauce-pan. Place the heart on top of them, and the remaining slice of pork on the heart, add the water, and dredge with salt, pepper, and flour. Bake slowly for two hours, basting frequently. Add the flour, mixed with a little cold water, in the course of the last half hour. Take off the cloth, place the heart on a platter, and strain the gravy over it.

SHEEP'S HEARTS.

Split the hearts, and wash and wipe them. Dredge with salt and pepper, and broil, over a clear fire, ten minutes. Season with butter, and serve. They may be prepared and roasted the same as the beef's heart; or they can be cut into small slices, and covered with hot water and simmered two hours. For six hearts take one quart of water, three cloves, two table spoonfuls of butter and two of flour. Simmer the hearts in the water with the cloves for one hour and a half. Rub the butter and flour together, and stir into the gravy. Season with salt and pepper, and simmer half an hour longer.

KIDNEYS.

Cook all kinds of kidneys the same as sheep's hearts. Hearts and kidneys must be cooked either a great deal or a very little, — that is, either rare, or until very well done ; or, in other words, not long enough to harden the albumen and fibrine, or a considerable time after the hardening has taken place.

BAKED LIVER.

Three pounds of beef liver or any other kind, quarter of a pound of salt pork, one onion, half a cupful of chopped carrot, the same quantity of chopped turnip, one pint and a half of water, two table-spoonfuls of flour, salt and pepper to taste. Cut the pork into thin slices, and spread part on the bottom of a deep baking-pan. Spread the vegetables on the pork, and dredge with salt and pepper. Now put in the liver, and lay the remainder of the pork over it. Add the water, and place in a moderate oven. Baste every fifteen minutes with the water in the pan, and salt, pepper, and flour. When the dish has been cooking one hour and a half, add the flour, mixed with a little cold water, and one table-spoonful of vinegar. Cook half an hour longer. Place the liver in a dish, and pour the gravy over it. Serve hot.

FRIED LIVER.

Cut the liver into slices about half an inch thick. Cover these with boiling water, and let them stand ten minutes. For every half pound of liver put two table-spoonfuls of drippings in the frying-pan, and when hot put in the meat. Cook *slowly* for eight minutes, seasoning with salt and pepper, and then remove from the pan. Put enough drippings in the pan to make two table-spoonfuls ; when hot add two table-spoonfuls of flour, and stir until brown ; then add one pint of cold water, and stir until it boils. Season with salt and pepper, and, after simmering five minutes, add one teaspoonful of vinegar. Pour the gravy over the liver, and serve. Cooking liver rapidly makes it hard. Lemon juice may be used instead of the vinegar. A table-spoonful of capers improves the sauce.

BOILED FISH.

Have boiling water enough to cover the fish. Salt it, and add one table-spoonful of vinegar to every two quarts of water. Dip a cloth in cold water, and lay the fish in it. Fold the cloth, and pin it together. Place in the boiling water, and just simmer until the fish is done ; then lift out the cloth, and roll the fish out of it and on to the dish on which it is to be served. A cod weighing four or six pounds will cook in thirty minutes ; four or six pounds of halibut will need forty-five minutes ; mackerel will require twenty minutes. A portion of a large fish, if of a cubical shape, will require half as long again for cooking as will the same quantity if of greater length and less thickness, or as will a small fish weighing the same number of pounds. Serve butter, tomato, egg, or milk sauce with boiled fish.

FRIED FISH.

The best way to fry fish is to have fat enough in the kettle to float the fish. This is not always convenient therefore, the next best mode will be explained. Pork fat gives a particularly nice flavor to fish; so, when it is liked, and is not beyond your means, it is much the best thing to use for frying. Beef and other drippings, cotton-seed oil, and lard are also good. Have the fish cut in small, flat pieces, and after seasoning these with salt and pepper dip them in a mixture of Indian meal and flour, or in bread or cracker crumbs. Have the bottom of the frying-pan covered to the depth of about a fourth of an inch with fat. When this is hot put in the fish, and fry until brown on one side; then turn, and brown on the other. If the fish be cut an inch thick it will take twelve minutes to fry it. Mackerel, trout, and other small fish should only be split, not cut.

BROILED FISH.

Fish for broiling should be small, or, if large, like halibut and salmon, should be cut about an inch thick. Season with salt and pepper. After rubbing the double broiler with a bit of pork or butter, lay the fish in it, and fasten the two parts together. Broil over or before clear coals until brown on the inside; then turn, and broil more slowly on the skin side. A thick mackerel will take twelve minutes; a slice of halibut or salmon, cut about an inch thick, will require from twelve to fifteen minutes; a split cod will broil in about the same time. As soon as the fish is done, turn back the side of the broiler that comes next the skin, and, placing over the fish a dish that has been warming, turn over broiler and dish simultaneously. The fish will thus be made to rest on the dish, skin side down and perfectly whole. Season with salt, pepper, and butter.

SALT FISH IN CREAM.

One pint of salt fish, one pint of milk, one tablespoonful of butter, one of flour, salt and pepper to taste. Cover the fish with cold water, and let it soak over night. In the morning pour off the water and add the milk to the fish. Let this heat slowly. Keep at the boiling point, without allowing it to actually boil, for half an hour. Rub the butter and flour together, and stir in with the fish and milk in the sauce-pan. Cook ten minutes. Season with salt and pepper.

SALT FISH WITH PORK.

Cut two large slices of pork into dice, and fry slowly until brown. Break a pint of cooked salt fish into flakes, and add to the pork. Stir over the fire until very hot. If you like the flavor, a table-spoonful of chopped onion may be fried with the pork before the fish is added.

MACARONI PIE.

Quarter of a pound of macaroni, one pound of pork sausage, salt, pepper, one cupful of bread crumbs. Break the macaroni into small pieces, and put in a sauce-pan with two quarts of boiling water. Boil twenty minutes. Put a layer of the cooked macaroni in a deep dish, and after dredging with salt and pepper add some of the water in which it was cooked; then add a layer of sausage, which has been cut into thin slices. Continue in this way until the macaroni and sausage are used; then cover with the bread crumbs. Bake one hour in a moderate oven. One pint of the water in which the macaroni was boiled should be used in preparing the dish, if you like it very moist; less will answer. Any kind of cold meat can be chopped and used in this way with boiled macaroni, cold ham and tongue being particularly nice. When white meats are used, thicken the pint of water with one table-spoonful of flour worked with one table-spoonful of butter.

WARMING COLD MEATS.

Unless cold meat is to be served in a stew, it should be cooked but little in reheating. One of the best modes of warming any kind of meat is in a gravy. Cut the meat into nice pieces, and season with salt and pepper. Put the bones and bits of gristle in a sauce-pan with cold water, and boil gently one or two hours. Put two table-spoonfuls of butter or drippings in a sauce-pan, and when hot add a heaping table-spoonful of dry flour. Stir until a rich brown; then add a pint of the broth, and cook five minutes. Season with salt and pepper. Add the meat, and simmer until it is heated through. This sauce is enough for three pints of meat. The dish may be varied by adding to the meat one teaspoonful or more of curry powder, by adding one cupful of tomatoes to the sauce, or by frying one onion with the butter or drippings before the flour is added. When the meat is white the flour can be cooked with the butter until it bubbles, but it must not brown; then a pint of milk can be used in place of the broth.

COTTAGER'S PIE.

Make a sauce as directed for cold meats. Add three pints of cold meat cut in small, thin bits, and put in a deep dish. Cover with one quart of mashed potato, and brown in the oven.

WARMING COLD FISH.

All kinds of cold fish can be warmed in a white sauce, and be served in it in a border of plain or mashed potatoes; or the fish may be added to the sauce, put in a deep dish, covered with bread crumbs, and browned in the oven; or it may be covered with mashed potato, instead of the crumbs, and browned.

Sauce for one quart of cold fish: one pint of milk, one table-spoonful of butter, one of flour, salt, pepper. Let the milk come to the boiling point. Rub the butter and flour together until smooth, and stir into the boiling milk. Boil three minutes. Season with salt and pepper. Add the fish, and simmer until hot.

COLD POTATOES.

Cold boiled potatoes, if properly prepared, make a pleasant addition to any meal. The common way is to fry — or, rather, soak — them in fat; and they come to the table, some hard and some soft, and all greasy. Use as little fat as possible in warming over potatoes, and cook them only long enough to heat them thoroughly. Here are several modes of preparing them : —

1. Cut the potatoes into thin slices. Season with salt and pepper, and chop a little. For one quart of potato put a large table-spoonful of butter, or any kind of sweet drippings, in the frying-pan, and when hot add the potatoes. Stir and cut with a knife until they are thoroughly heated. Turn into a warm dish, and serve immediately.

2. Put one large table-spoonful of sweet drippings in the frying-pan, and, when hot, add one table-spoonful of chopped onion. Fry till of a light straw color; then add one quart of chopped and seasoned potatoes. Stir frequently with a fork until *hot*. Serve in a warm dish.

3. Put half a pint of milk in the frying-pan, and while it is heating rub together one table-spoonful of butter and one teaspoonful of flour. As soon as the milk boils, stir the flour and butter into it. Boil up, and season with salt and pepper. Now add a pint and a half of cold potatoes, cut into rather large dice, and seasoned with salt and pepper.

4. Put one cupful of milk in the frying-pan, and when it boils add one table-spoonful of butter, some salt and pepper, and a quart of rather finely-chopped potatoes, seasoned with salt and pepper. Stir with a fork until hot. Serve immediately in a hot dish.

VEGETABLE HASH.

Use all kinds of vegetables left from a boiled dinner. After cutting the potatoes, carrots, turnips, beets, and parsnips into slices, put them with the cabbage, and either chop in a tray or cut with a knife. Dredge with salt, pepper, and a little flour. For each quart of the vegetable mixture use a tablespoonful of drippings. Put all in the frying-pan, cover, and heat slowly. If there be a large quantity of cabbage it will make the hash moist enough, but if not a few spoonfuls of the water in which the vegetables were boiled will be an improvement. Be careful not to get too much carrot in the hash. A very little gives it a pleasing flavor, but a large quantity destroys the flavor of the other vegetables. Have the vegetables as nearly as possible in this proportion : six parts cabbage, four parts turnip, four parts potato, three parts beet, two parts parsnip, one part carrot. Of course, in making a hash like this, one has to use what is left, and these proportions are not always possible. Any other kind of vegetable that you may have can be used also.

COLD VEGETABLES.

CABBAGE. — Cold cabbage, chopped, and warmed with one tablespoonful of pork fat or butter to each quart of cabbage, is nice served on toast. Boil two quarts of pared potatoes, and when they are done drain off the water, mash well, and add one tablespoonful of butter, one quart of chopped cabbage, and salt and pepper to taste. Stir over the fire until hot. Or heat one quart of cold cabbage with one table-spoonful of drippings and two table-spoonfuls of vinegar.

BEETS, ETC. — Cold beets can be cut into slices and covered with vinegar; or they can be cut into dice, and warmed in a sauce made with half a cupful of milk thickened with half a teaspoonful of flour rubbed with one teaspoonful of butter. This is enough sauce for a pint of beets.

Carrots, beans, and other cooked vegetables can be served in the same manner.

STEAMED RICE.

One cupful of rice, three cupfuls of cold water, one teaspoonful of salt. Wash the rice in three waters, and put it and the salt and water in a bowl that will hold about three pints. Steam one hour. When ready to serve, turn into a warm vegetable dish. The rice will keep its shape if taken out gently, and seems especially palatable served in this way.

DINNER APPLE SAUCE.

Put two quarts of pared and quartered apples in a deep earthen dish, and sprinkle over them one teaspoonful of cinnamon, half a cupful of sugar, one third of a cupful of molasses, and one cupful of water. Cut one table-spoonful of butter into little bits, and sprinkle over the top. Cover the dish with a large plate, and bake in a slow oven for one hour. All sugar or all molasses may be used. The quantity named does not give much sweetness. More sugar may be used if the sauce be liked sweet.

RHUBARB SAUCE.

Strip the thin skin from the rhubarb. Cut the stalk into pieces about an inch long. Wash, and put in a stew-pan, covering with boiling water. In an hour pour off the water. To each quart of rhubarb add one fourth of a cupful of water and one large cupful of sugar. Stew up quickly, and cool in an earthen dish. This gives a light green sauce. It may be put in an earthen dish, covered with a plate, and baked one hour in a moderate oven. By this mode of preparation the pieces are preserved unbroken.

BROWN BETTY PUDDING.

One cupful of bread crumbs, two cupfuls of finely-chopped tart apples, half a cupful of brown sugar, one teaspoonful of cinnamon, one table-spoonful of butter cut into little bits. Butter a deep dish, and put a layer of apple on the bottom; then sprinkle with sugar, cinnamon, and butter, and cover with bread crumbs. Put in another layer of apple, and proceed as before, until all the ingredients are used, having a layer of crumbs on top. Cover the dish, and bake forty-five minutes in a moderate oven. Remove the cover, and brown the top of the pudding. Place the dish in a clean one, or pin a napkin around it. Serve with sugar and milk.

TROY PUDDING.

Half a cupful each of chopped suet, chopped raisins, molasses, and milk, two cupfuls of flour, half a teaspoonful of soda, half a teaspoonful of salt. Dissolve the soda in the milk, after which mix all the ingredients together. Turn into a buttered brown bread tin, or a three-pint basin, and steam two hours. Serve hot, with a cold or hot sauce.

HUCKLEBERRY PUDDING.

One and a half cupfuls of sour milk, one and a half of molasses, five and a half of flour, one teaspoonful of soda, half a teaspoonful of salt, one quart of berries. Dissolve the soda in the milk, and mix with the molasses and salt. Beat the flour into this mixture, and add the berries. Steam three hours. These quantities will make one large or two small puddings. Serve with a sweet sauce. Sweet milk can be used if you have not the sour.

SUET INDIAN PUDDING.

Two cupfuls of sour milk, one of chopped suet, one and a half of granulated corn meal, one teaspoonful of soda, one of salt. Put the molasses, milk, and salt together. Dissolve the soda in two table-spoonfuls of hot water, and add it and the meal to the mixture; then add the suet. Steam three hours. Serve with a sweet sauce. A pint of chopped apples or of berries may be added with the suet.

BATTER PUDDING.

One pint of milk, one of flour, one of berries, three eggs. Beat the eggs well, but not the yolks and whites separately, and add the milk to them. Pour gradually upon the flour, beating well; then add the berries. Turn into a buttered earthen dish, and bake one hour. Serve with a sweet sauce.

BAKED TAPIOCA PUDDING.

One quart of milk, one small cupful of tapioca, one cupful of cold water, three eggs, one teaspoonful of salt, an orange, half a cupful of sugar. Wash the tapioca in plenty of water, and let it soak in the cupful of cold water for one hour, at the end of which time add the milk to it, and cook in the double boiler for an hour. Let it cool. Beat the salt, sugar, and eggs together, and add to the cooked tapioca and milk. Turn into a pudding dish. Cut the orange into thin slices, and lay these over the top. Bake forty minutes in a moderate oven. One teaspoonful of lemon or vanilla extract, or a slight grating of nutmeg, may be used instead of the orange. If you are in a hurry for the pudding the eggs and sugar may be added while the mixture is hot. It will then take from fifteen to twenty minutes to bake. Adding the eggs to the cold mixture will, however, give you a smoother and firmer pudding.

BOILED TAPIOCA PUDDING.

One large cupful of tapioca, two cupfuls of cold water, one quart of milk, one teaspoonful of salt. Wash the tapioca, and soak it for one hour in the two cupfuls of water. Add the milk, and cook in the double boiler one hour. When it has been cooking three quarters of an hour, add the salt, stirring well. This pudding is nice either hot or cold. To be served with sugar and milk.

OATMEAL PUDDING.

Make oatmeal mush, as directed on page 87. Turn into a mould or bowl, and set away to cool. To be eaten with sugar and milk.

Another way to make the pudding is to stir one cupful of oatmeal and one teaspoonful of salt into one quart of boiling water, and cook one hour; then add one generous pint of milk, and cook thirty minutes longer. Turn into a mould, and set away to cool. The oatmeal can be cooked in the double boiler, and will then require one third less water. It need not be stirred after the first hour.

HOMINY PUDDING.

Cook the hominy as directed on page 87. Turn into a mould, and set away to cool. Serve with sugar and milk.

CORN-STARCH PUDDING.

One quart of milk, four table-spoonfuls of corn-starch, one teaspoonful of salt. Put the milk on to boil, reserving half a cupful to mix with the corn-starch. When the milk boils, add the corn-starch, mixed with the cold milk and salt. Beat well, and cook twelve minutes. Serve with sugar and milk. This is nice hot or cold. If you choose, you may add one third of a cupful of sugar and one teaspoonful of lemon or vanilla extract; or the sugar and a grating of nutmeg, if you intend serving it cold. The sugar and flavor can be added when you take it from the fire, being careful to beat them in well. Or you may add a tumbler of bright jelly just as you take the pudding from the fire.

HOT FARINA PUDDING.

One quart of milk, four heaping table-spoonfuls of farina, one teaspoonful of salt. Put all the milk but half a cupful on to boil. When it boils, add the farina and salt, mixed with the cold milk. Cook one hour, stirring frequently. Serve with sugar and milk.

COLD FARINA PUDDING.

One quart of milk, one teaspoonful of salt, three table-spoonfuls of farina. Mix the farina, salt, and half a cupful of the milk together. Let the remainder of the milk come to the boiling point, and stir the farina into it. Cook one hour; then add three table-spoonfuls of sugar and one teaspoonful of vanilla or lemon flavor, or a little nutmeg. Turn into a mould, and set away to cool. The sugar and flavor may be omitted, and one tumbler of jelly stirred in instead. When the pudding is cold, serve with sugar and milk.

GINGERBREAD PUDDING.

One cupful of molasses, one of milk (sour or sweet), three of flour, one table-spoonful of drippings, one table-spoonful of cinnamon, one teaspoonful of soda, half a teaspoonful of salt, one table-spoonful of vinegar. Mix together the molasses, seasonings, and drippings. Dissolve the soda in the milk, and add to the molasses; then add the flour, and finally the vinegar. Bake in shallow pans, and serve hot with cream sauce. (See page 80.) If the mixture be an inch deep it will take twenty minutes to bake in a moderate oven.

RICE AND APPLE PUDDING.

Two quarts of pared and quartered apples, one cupful of rice, one table-spoonful of salt. Wash the rice, and boil in one pint of water for ten minutes. Wring a pudding cloth out of hot water, and spread on a flat dish. Over the cloth spread the rice, and sprinkle the salt over it; then spread on the apples. Tie very tightly, plunge into boiling water, and boil constantly for one hour. Take up the pudding, and plunge into cold water for an instant. Cut the string, and turn the pudding into a deep dish. It should come out in the form of a ball. Serve with molasses sauce. Less apple may be used, if you prefer, and any kind of sweet sauce will be good with this pudding.

STEAMED FRUIT PUDDING.

Three pints of pared and quartered apples, two thirds of a cupful of sugar, one pint of water, a little cinnamon or nutmeg. Put the apples and other ingredients in a deep tin basin holding about three pints, and place this on the stove, keeping it there until the pudding has been heated to the boiling point. While the apples are cooking make some biscuit, using half the quantities given in the rule in this appendix. The dough should be rolled down to the thickness of about half an inch. The surface of the boiling apple is to be covered with the dough, and then the pudding is to be covered with a buttered pan like that in which it is cooking. Boil gently twelve minutes. Remove the upper pan, and place the lower on a china dish, and send to the table. Blueberries or rhubarb may be used instead of the apple.

BAKED INDIAN PUDDING.

Five pints of milk, thirteen table-spoonfuls of Indian meal, one cupful of molasses, one teaspoonful of salt. Let two quarts of the milk heat to the boiling point, and pour it gradually on the meal. Put the mixture in the double boiler, and boil half an hour, stirring frequently; then add the salt and molasses. Let the mixture stand until blood warm. Turn into a buttered pudding dish, and add a pint of cold milk, but do not stir. Bake three hours in a slow oven.

SNOW PUDDING.

One pint of boiling water, two lemons, half a cupful of sugar, four table-spoonfuls of corn-starch, half a cupful of cold water, the whites of four eggs. Put the boiling water in the double boiler, with lemon juice and sugar. Add the corn-starch, which has been mixed with the cold water. Cook ten minutes. Beat the whites of the eggs to a stiff froth, and after removing the boiling mixture from the fire add them to it. Put in moulds, to cool. Serve with a soft custard, made of one pint of milk, the yolks of the four eggs, one whole egg, and one fourth of a cupful of sugar. Beat the eggs and sugar together; add the milk to them, and stir in the double boiler until the mixture begins to thicken. When it looks as thick at the edge of the spoon as in the centre, it is done. Season with lemon or vanilla, and serve cold.

SUNDAY PUDDING.

One quart of sifted flour, one coffee-cupful of stoned and chopped raisins, half a teacupful each of molasses and sugar, two teacupfuls of sour milk, a teacupful of chopped suet, one teaspoonful of salt, one of soda. Mix all the ingredients together, adding the soda, which has been dissolved in three table-spoonfuls of hot water, last. Steam from three to five hours. Three will do, but five makes it richer.

BAKED RICE PUDDING.

Two thirds of a cupful of rice, half a cupful of sugar, one teaspoonful of salt, a generous quart of milk. Wash the rice, and mix with other ingredients. Bake slowly one hour, stirring twice during the first half hour. This pudding is good without a sauce, but is very nice with currant or other jelly.

HASTY PUDDING.

Mix a pint of Indian meal with one of cold water, and stir into a quart of boiling water. Place the stew-pan on the fire until the mixture boils, stirring often; then place in a basin of boiling water, and cook two hours.

BLANC-MANGE.

Sea-moss farine is one of the simplest, cheapest, and most healthful preparations in the market for making blanc-mange. Follow the rule closely, and you will always be sure of perfect success. One quart of milk, one scant table-spoonful of farine, three table-spoonfuls of sugar, one large teaspoonful of vanilla or emon extract. Put the milk in a double boiler, and sprinkle in the farine. Stir well, and heat slowly, stirring often. When it is a little frothy on top add the sugar, and cook ten minutes longer. Take from the fire, and add the flavor. Turn into moulds, and set away to cool. When cold, serve with sugar and cream or milk. Cups or bowls will answer to cool it in, if you have no moulds.

COLD SAUCE.

Four table-spoonfuls of sugar, half a table-spoonful of butter, one teaspoonful of hot water, half a teaspoonful of vanilla extract. Beat the butter to a cream. Add the sugar gradually, and the water and flavor, and when smooth and creamy put in a small dish, and grate nutmeg on top. To be served with any kind of hot pudding.

MOLASSES SAUCE.

One cupful of molasses, one table-spoonful of butter, half a cupful of water, half a cupful of sugar, a little nutmeg, the juice of one lemon or one table-spoonful of vinegar, one teaspoonful of corn-starch. Mix the corn-starch with a little cold water, and add it to the other ingredients. Cook all together twenty minutes.

PLAIN PIE CRUST.

One quart of flour, one teaspoonful of baking-powder, one cupful of lard or butter, one table-spoonful of salt, one of sugar, one cupful and a quarter of water. Mix the salt, sugar, and baking-powder thoroughly with the flour; then rub in half the lard or butter. Add the water, stirring with a knife. When the paste is a smooth ball place it on a *lightly*-floured board, and roll down to the thickness of about one fourth of an inch. Spread half of the remaining shortening on it, and sprinkle *lightly* with flour. Fold up, and roll down to the thickness of a quarter of an inch. Add the remainder of the butter, fold up and roll down as before. Now roll up again, and set away to cool; or it can be used immediately. This is enough for four pies of medium size. Beef suet can be used instead of lard or butter. The suet may be tried out and cooled, or it can be chopped very fine, and used the same as the lard or butter. Everything should be as cold as possible when making the crust and using it. Pies ought not to be given preference over puddings, which are not only more easily made, but are cheaper and more healthful.

APPLE PIE.

Cover a deep pie-plate with plain paste, and fill with pared and sliced apples. Cover with paste rolled a little thicker than for the under crust. Press the edges together, and bake the pie in a moderate oven for half an hour. As soon as it is cooked, lift the cover off, and add to the apples bits of butter, if you like, and half a cupful of sugar dissolved in a few table-spoonfuls of water. Grate a little nutmeg over the whole mixture. Return the cover and set away to cool. The amount of sugar necessary will vary. If the apples be very sour more sugar will be required than the quantity given above, and if they be mild less. Evaporated apples can be used instead of the green ones. Wash one pint of them, and soak over night in a little more than enough cold water to cover. In making the pie, proceed the same as with the green apples, adding to the fruit, however, three table-spoonfuls of the water in which it was soaked.

RHODE ISLAND PIE.

One quart of pared and sliced apple, one fourth of a cupful of sugar, one fourth of a cupful of water, one third of a cupful of molasses, half a teaspoonful of cinnamon. Put these ingredients in a deep pie-plate, and cover with a plain crust. Bake from thirty to forty minutes. When ready to serve, run a knife between the crust and the plate, place a large plate on top, and turn both plates simultaneously. This leaves the crust on the bottom and the filling on top.

RHUBARB PIE.

One cupful of pared and chopped rhubarb, one scant cupful of sugar, one egg, well beaten, half a teaspoonful of flour. Line a pie-plate with plain paste. Mix the rhubarb, sugar, flour, and egg together, and turn into the plate. Cover with a thin crust, pressing the edges of the paste together, and bake forty minutes.

LEMON PIE.

Three eggs, one cupful of sugar, one lemon, one cupful of boiling water, one table-spoonful of corn-starch, one table-spoonful of powdered sugar. Mix the corn-starch with three table-spoonfuls of cold water, and pour the boiling water upon it. Beat together the sugar, lemon juice and rind, and one white and the yolks of the eggs. Pour the corn-starch mixture on this. Have a deep plate lined with plain paste, and pour the combined mixtures into it. Bake slowly for thirty-five minutes. When the pie is nearly cold, beat the two remaining egg whites to a stiff froth, and then beat the powdered sugar in with them. Brown slowly in a rather cool oven.

CUSTARD PIE.

Line a deep pie-plate with plain paste. Beat two eggs with two table-spoonfuls of sugar, one fourth of a teaspoonful of salt, and a little nutmeg. Beat with a spoon, and not too light. Add a scant pint of milk. Stir well, and turn the custard into the plate. Bake in a moderate oven until firm in the centre.

SQUASH PIE.

One *small* cupful of stewed and strained squash, one *large* cupful of boiling milk, one table-spoonful of powdered cracker, one fourth of a cupful of sugar, half a teaspoonful of salt, one fourth of a teaspoonful of cinnamon, a slight grating of nutmeg. Mix the seasonings and cracker with the squash. Pour the *boiling* milk on this mixture, which let stand until it cools. Pour into a deep plate that has been lined with plain paste, and bake *slowly* one hour

DOUGHNUTS.

One quart of flour, one cupful of sugar, three teaspoonfuls of baking-powder, two eggs, half a teaspoonful of salt, a little nutmeg, one cupful of milk. Mix all the dry ingredients together, and rub through a sieve; then add the beaten eggs and the milk, stirring well with a spoon. Flour the board, and put about one fourth of the mixture on it in the shape of a ball. Roll down to the thickness of about half an inch, and cut into round cakes. If you have no regular cutter, cut a small piece from the centre of the cakes with a thimble. Fry in a deep kettle of lard or drippings. Handle the dough as little as possible; working flour into it toughens the doughnuts. If you like them cracked open on one side, do not turn them while frying until they are cooked on the under side. They will cook in about four minutes.

MOLASSES COOKIES.

One cupful of molasses, half a cupful of brown sugar, one cupful of lard or nice drippings, one teaspoonful of soda, one cupful of cold water, half a teaspoonful of salt, one heaping teaspoonful of ginger, enough flour to make stiff for rolling. Mix the molasses and lard together, and add the salt and ginger. Dissolve the soda in the water, and add to the other ingredients. Stir in the flour, and when a firm batter has been formed put part of it on the floured board, and roll down to the thickness of about an eighth of an inch. Cut into round cakes, and bake in a quick oven.

PLAIN SUGAR COOKIES.

One cupful of sugar, half a cupful of butter, lard, or drippings, half a cupful of milk, one teaspoonful and a half of baking-powder, half a teaspoonful of salt, a little nutmeg, flour enough to make stiff for rolling.

Make and bake the same as the molasses cookies. Always use as little flour as possible in making cookies.

SUET CAKE.

One cupful of milk, two and a half cupfuls of flour, two thirds of a cupful of molasses, two thirds of a cupful of sugar, one cupful of chopped suet, one egg, one heaping teaspoonful of soda, one even teaspoonful of cream of tartar, one table-spoonful of vinegar, spice to taste, or not, as you please. Beat the egg first, and add the molasses and sugar, beating well again. Mix the soda and milk together. Mix the flour and cream of tartar together, and add to them the other ingredients, the suet and vinegar being taken last. Bake thirty minutes in shallow pans. The quantities given are sufficient for two sheets.

SPICE CAKE.

Half a cupful each of molasses, milk, sugar, butter, and raisins or currants, two and a half cupfuls of sifted flour, one egg, half a teaspoonful of clove, one teaspoonful of cinnamon, half a teaspoonful of soda. Beat the egg, sugar, and butter together. Add the molasses and the milk, in which should be dissolved the soda; then add the flour and spices, and finally the fruit. Bake half an hour in shallow pans in a moderate oven. This is a good cake without the fruit. Two sheets can be made with the quantities named.

POVERTY CAKE.

One cupful of sugar, two and a half cupfuls of sifted flour, one large table-spoonful of butter (lard or drippings will do), one teaspoonful of cream of tartar, half a teaspoonful of soda or one and a half teaspoonfuls of baking-powder, half a teaspoonful of salt, one cupful of milk. Have the butter soft, and rub it together with the sugar. Mix the soda with the flour, and rub through the sieve. Add the milk to the sugar and butter; then add the flour and a little nutmeg. Bake in shallow pans in a rather quick oven for twenty-five minutes. A few currants make a pleasant change. The quantities given will make two sheets.

SPICE BREAD.

Make bread according to the rule on page 69, and when it has risen work into it one cupful of brown sugar, half a cupful of butter or drippings, one tablespoonful of cinnamon, half a teaspoonful of clove, half a teaspoonful of allspice. Shape into loaves, and let these rise slowly for two hours. Bake one hour and a quarter. This bread keeps well, and takes the place of cake with children. A cupful each of raisins and currants makes a great improvement.

SWEDISH BREAD.

When yeast bread has risen and is ready for the pans, take one pint of the dough and roll it very thin. Spread over this one table-spoonful of cinnamon mixed with half a cupful of sugar. First moisten the sheet of bread with cold water, then sprinkle with the cinnamon and sugar. Roll very tight, and cut into slices with a sharp knife. Place the slices on well-greased tins. Let them rise one hour and a quarter, and bake them in a quick oven. If you like, spread the dough with butter instead of water.

PANCAKES.

Two eggs, two cupfuls of sour milk, one table-spoonful of butter, one teacupful of sugar, five cupfuls of flour, one teaspoonful of soda. Beat the eggs, and add them to the milk, sugar, and the butter, which must be melted. Stir this mixture into the flour. Dissolve the soda in three table-spoonfuls of hot water, and add to the batter the last thing. Have a deep kettle of boiling fat, and drop the mixture into it in half spoonfuls ; the spoon being first dipped in water or milk. Cook five minutes.

SPIDER CORN-CAKE.

One and two thirds cupfuls of meal, one third of a cupful of flour, two eggs, two cupfuls of sweet milk and one of sour, one fourth of a cupful of sugar, a small teaspoonful of soda, one teaspoonful of salt, a piece of butter half the size of an egg. Dissolve the soda in one cupful of the sweet milk. Beat the eggs light. Add the milk in which the soda is dissolved and also the sour milk to the dry ingredients, and then add the eggs. Have a large frying-pan very hot. Put the butter in it, greasing the sides well, and pour in the mixture. Now pour in the other cupful of sweet milk, but do not stir the cake. Place the frying-pan in a hot oven, and bake from twenty to twenty-five minutes.

BISCUIT.

One quart of unsifted flour, three teaspoonfuls of baking-powder, one table-spoonful of butter, lard, or drippings, one teaspoonful of salt, one table-spoonful of sugar, milk or water enough to make a soft dough (nearly a pint). Mix the dry ingredients together, and rub through a sieve ; add the wetting, and stir with a spoon until a smooth paste is formed. Sprinkle the board lightly with flour, and roll the dough down on it to the thickness of about half an inch. Cut into small cakes, and bake fifteen minutes in a *very* hot oven.

STEAMED INDIAN BREAD.

Two cupfuls of sweet milk, one of sour, three of corn meal, one of flour, two thirds of a cupful of molasses, one teaspoonful of soda, one of salt, one tablespoonful of vinegar. Mix together the flour, meal, and salt. Dissolve the soda in the sweet milk. Mix the sour milk, molasses, and vinegar together. Add the soda and sweet milk to them, and stir all in with the meal and flour. Beat well, and turn into greased tins. Steam two hours.

INDEX.

Air, 1
Albuminous matter, 32
Analogy between the living body and a steam-engine, 26
Apple sauce, 110
Articles for the cooking room, 128
Baking powders, 55
Barley, 51
Beans, baked, 101
  stewed, 102
Beef olives, 90
  tea, 117
Beefsteak, 121
Boiling, 34
Bread, 46, 67
  aerated, 54
  biscuit, 170
  brown bread, 88
  Graham, 72
  hints on making, 52, 70
  leaven, 54
  pancakes, 170
  salt-rising bread, 54
  spiced bread, 169
  spider corn-cake, 170
  Swedish bread, 169
  yeast, 67
  yeast bread, 69
Broiling, 34, 78
Broth, chicken, 118
Buckwheat, 51
Burns, 124

Cake :
  corn-cake, spider, 170
  molasses cookies, 167
  gingerbread, 94
  pancakes, 170
  poverty cake, 168
  spice, 169
  sponge, 94
  suet, 168
  sugar cookies, 167
Carbon, 29
  compounds, 31
Carbonic acid, 2
Care of the house, 5
Chamber work, 16
Chicken broth, 118
Chocolate, 66
Chowders :
  chicken, 135
  clam, 133
  fish, 89, 134
  potato, 135
  tomato, 136
Classification of food, 31
Cocoa, 65
Coffee, 62
  boiled, 62
  filtered, 63
  steamed, 64
Cold fish, 151
  meats, 150
  potatoes, 151
  sauce, 163.

INDEX.

Cold vegetables, 153
Composition of the human body, 27
Condiments, 56
Constipation, cure for, 124
Cooking room, articles for, 128
Corn bread, 170
    tea, 119
Corn-starch pudding, 158
Cottager's pie, 151
Custard pie, 166
Custards, baked, 115
    steamed, 115
Digestion, remarks on, 22
Doughnuts, 166
Dumplings, 75
Egg-nog, 122
Eggs, 36
    boiled, 36
    dropped, 37
    omelets, 37, 112
    poached, 37
Elements of the human body, 29
Filling for cream pies, 95
Fires, 22
Fish, 38
    baked, 82
    boiled, 147
    broiled, 78, 148
    clams, 38
    clam chowder, 133
        soup, 133
    cold fish, to warm, 151
    fish balls, 86
        chowder, 89, 134
        hash, 86
        stew, 140
    fried fish, 148
    lobsters, 38
    mussels, 38
    oyster soup, 113
    oysters, 38
        boiled, 114
        fried, 114
        scalloped, 113
        stewed, 113

Fish — salt fish, 39
    chowder, 134
    in cream, 149
    with pork, 149
Flavors, 59
Flour gruel, 122
Fruit, 45
Frying, 35
Gruel, flour, 122
    Indian meal, 119
Hoarseness, cure for, 123
Hominy, 87, 158
Housework, 14
Human body, the, 26
Indian corn, 49
    meal gruel, 119
Iron rust, 20
Ironing, 21
Lace curtains, 20
Lamb chops, 121
Lamps, 24
Leaven, 54
Lemonade, 43
Lettuce, 43
Lungs, drink for the, 123
Macaroni, 114
    pie, 149
Meats, 33
    barley stew, 137
    beef's heart, 145
    beefsteak, braised, 141
    beef olives, 87
    beef stew, 74
    chicken chowder, 135
    corned beef stew, 138
    cottager's pie, 151
    flank of beef, rolled, 144
    fricassee of cold meat, 143
        of veal, 143
    Irish stew, 138
    kidneys, 146
    liver, baked, 146
        fried, 146
    macaroni pie, 149
    meat hash, 85
    mutton chops, 121
        stew, 138

INDEX.

Meats — *pot-au-feu*, 81
  roasting, 76
  sausage stew, 139
  sheep's hearts, 145
  stewed beef, 141
  veal, fricassee of, 143
    olives, 91
    pot pie, 142
    stew, 139
  warming cold meats, 150
Milk, 35
Mint, 57
Muffins, 72
  Graham, 79
Mustard, 57
Mutton chops, 121
Nitrogen, 2
  compounds, 31
Oatmeal, 50
  gruel, 119
  mush, 87
Olives, beef, 90
  veal, 91
Omelets, 37, 112
Order of housework, 14
Oxygen, 1
Pancakes, 170
Pears, baked, 110
Pepper, 56
Pie crust, 163
Pies :
  apple, 164
  cottager's, 151
  cream, 95
  custard, 166
  lemon, 165
  Rhode Island, 165
  rhubarb, 165
  squash, 166
  Washington, 95
Plum porridge, 119
Potatoes, 41
  boiled, 79
  cold, 151
Poultry, 103
  chicken broth, 118
    chowder, 135

Poultry — roast chicken, 104
  duck, 105
  goose, 105
  grouse, 106
  partridge, 106
  small birds, 106
  turkey, 103
Puddings :
  apple dowdy, 92
  batter pudding, 156
  blanc-mange, 162
  bread pudding, 80
  brown Betty, 155
  corn-starch, 158
  custard, 115
  farina, 159
  fruit, 160
  gingerbread, 159
  hasty, 162
  hominy, 158
  huckleberry, 156
  Indian, 83, 161
  minute, 87
  oatmeal, 158
  rice, baked, 92, 162
    boiled, 91
    steamed, 154
  rice and apple, 160
  snow, 161
  suet Indian, 156
  Sunday, 162
  tapioca, baked, 157
    boiled, 157
  Troy, 155
  whitpot, 95
Quaker omelet, 112
Rice, 51, 154
  coffee, 121
Roasting, 34, 76
Rye, 50
Sack posset, 118
Sage, 57
Salad dressings, 98
Salads, 43, 98
  chicken, 101
  lettuce, 100
  lobster, 101

Salads — potato, 100
    vegetable, 99
Salt, 56
    meats, 35
Sauces :
    apple, 110, 154
    baked pears, 110
    coddled apples, 111
    cranberry, 111
    rhubarb, 154
    stewed prunes, 111
    for meats, fish, and vegetables :
        bread, 108
        caper, 108
        celery, 108
        cream, 108
        drawn butter, 107
        egg, 107
        Hollandaise, 109
        milk, 110
        mint, 108
        oyster, 107
        tomato, 109
    for puddings :
        cold, 163
        cream, 80
        lemon, 93
        molasses, 163
        vinegar, 88
Shells, 66
Sick-room cookery, 116
Soups :
    bean, 131
    clam chowder, 133
        soup, 133
    chicken chowder, 135
    onion soup, 131
    oyster, 113
    pea, 130
    potato chowder, 135
    pot-au-feu, 81
    salt fish chowder, 134
    shin of beef soup, 132
    tomato chowder, 136
        soup, 83
    vegetable, 132

Spice, 58
Starching, 20
Steamed rice, 154
Stewing, 34
Stews :
    barley, 137
    beef, 74
    corned beef, 138
    fish, 140
    Irish, 138
    mutton, 138
    parsnip, 137
    sausage, 139
    veal, 139
    vegetable, 141
Summer savory, 57
Sweet marjoram, 57
Tea, 61
Thyme, 57
Toast, cream, 121
    milk, 115
Vegetables, 41, 95
    beans, 42, 92
        baked, 101
        stewed, 102
    beets, 41, 96, 153
    cabbage, 42, 96, 153
    carrots, 43, 96, 153
    celery, 44, 96
    cucumbers, 44
    onions, 42, 96
    parsnips, 43, 96, 137
    peas, 42, 96
    potatoes, 41, 96, 151
    squash, 41, 96
    sweet potatoes, 42, 96
    tomatoes, 42, 96
    turnips, 41, 96
Ventilation, 5
Washing clothes, 18
    floors and tables, 17
Water, 8
    cresses, 44
Watery vapor, 3
Whey, sour milk, 120
    vinegar, 120
    wine, 119

www.ingramcontent.com/pod-product-compliance
Lightning Source LLC
Chambersburg PA
CBHW031438160426

43195CB00010BB/776